FINDING JOY

FINDING JOY

A PRACTICAL SPIRITUAL GUIDE TO HAPPINESS

DANNEL I. SCHWARTZ

with Mark Hass

Jewish Lights Publishing

Woodstock, Vermont

Finding Joy
A Practical Spiritual Guide to Happiness
© 1996 by Dannel I. Schwartz

Library of Congress Cataloging-in-Publication Data

Schwartz, Dannel I.
Finding joy: a practical spiritual guide to happiness / Dannel I. Schwartz with Mark Hass.
p. cm.
Includes bibliographical references.
ISBN 1-879045-53-2
1. Joy—Religious aspects—Judaism. 2. Judaism.
I. Hass, Mark, 1953– . II. Title.
BM645.J67S34 1996
296.7'4—dc20   96-9507
                                CIP

10 9 8 7 6 5 4 3 2 1

ISBN 1-879045-53-2 (Hardcover)

Manufactured in the United States of America

Book and jacket designed by Glenn Suokko

Published by Jewish Lights Publishing
A Division of LongHill Partners, Inc.
P.O. Box 237
Sunset Farm Offices, Rte. 4
Woodstock, Vermont 05091
Tel: (802) 457-4000 Fax: (802) 457-4004

To the happiest person I know, my wife,
Suzi Romanik Schwartz.
Her love, her smile, her hope and her talent
have lit up my life with joy.

— Dannel I. Schwartz

For Sherry. For Happiness.

— Mark Hass

CONTENTS

The Ten Sefirot

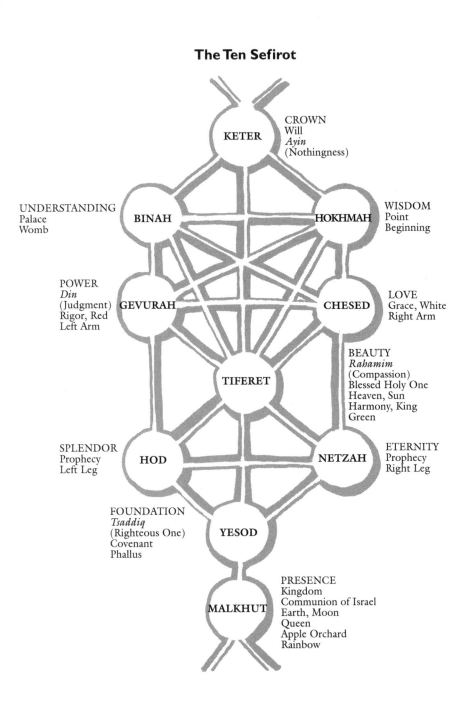

CROWN
Will
Ayin
(Nothingness)

KETER

UNDERSTANDING
Palace
Womb

BINAH

WISDOM
Point
Beginning

HOKHMAH

POWER
Din
(Judgment)
Rigor, Red
Left Arm

GEVURAH

LOVE
Grace, White
Right Arm

CHESED

BEAUTY
Rahamim
(Compassion)
Blessed Holy One
Heaven, Sun
Harmony, King
Green

TIFERET

SPLENDOR
Prophecy
Left Leg

HOD

ETERNITY
Prophecy
Right Leg

NETZAH

FOUNDATION
Tsaddiq
(Righteous One)
Covenant
Phallus

YESOD

PRESENCE
Kingdom
Communion of Israel
Earth, Moon
Queen
Apple Orchard
Rainbow

MALKHUT

ACKNOWLEDGMENTS

Being a mystic becomes doubly pleasurable when you can live it and teach it, too. And when the otherwise rational student becomes totally immersed in the deliciously non-rational world of the mystic and can see what his or her teacher sees, then the miracles of "teaching" and "learning" occur. To those of my students who saw even more than I saw and were the first to realize that *Finding Joy* should be a book I give my profound thanks.

I am sure that when one of the scribes was busily at work writing the text of Exodus, some editor appeared and said, "For God's sake! Fifteen plagues is overkill. Cut it to ten. The whole Bible will read better and you'll make your point." Behind every good author is an editor who can cut the one story too many and be the unbiased, impartial and practiced eye that keeps a book on target. This book is far from being the Bible, but it had Arthur Magida, who is one of the best. He cut some of the tales, but kept the meat of the book intact. His attention to detail and commitment to his craft made me proud to be part of the whole process.

Stuart Matlins, my publisher, deserves kind words for helping, early in the writing process, to set the tone for this volume. He correctly insisted that the voice of the teacher, the teller of tales, and the mystic be woven throughout the fabric of the book. As much as anyone, he helped give this book its final shape.

Most of all, thanks to my friend and partner, Mark Hass, who has been an integral part of this undertaking from the beginning and kept me believing in it. His capacity to create order from chaos and rescue a meaningful thought from a cliché is his God-given gift. His ability to manage the mystic's enigmas and solve some ancient riddles, and to force me into making them useful and usable in today's world, is really the spark that makes this book so unique.

And most importantly, both Mark and I are more than grateful to our wives, Suzi Romanik Schwartz and Sherry Hass. This labor of love would not have been possible without their support, patience and good humor through the late evenings and long weekends that were consumed by our writing process.

And one final thanks. This one to you, the reader, for joining me on this mystical journey.

Dannel Schwartz

INTRODUCTION

In our society, happiness is elusive, but in great demand.

Why can some of us find it in our day-to-day existence, even when that existence is a struggle? Why do others, despite apparent advantages, feel miserable? Is the answer in a diet, an exercise program, a crystal? That's unlikely, because happiness is not in what we eat, how we look or what we wear around our necks. Instead, it lies in a spiritual approach to living, an approach consistent with the teachings of the fundamental texts of Jewish mystical life, which hold remarkable insights for Jews and non-Jews alike who are searching for joy.

Unfortunately, those texts are rarely used today to shape a conceptual basis for making life happier. That's a shame, because the mystics offer some good, practical advice for happiness. The core concepts of Jewish mysticism are built on the belief that joy is possible and the world can be better appreciated if our lives have a spiritual focus. Making life more fulfilling and enjoyable, in fact, is the basis of any spiritual formula for living.

Finding Joy: A Practical Spiritual Guide to Happiness uses that guiding principle to explore the spiritual nature of the joy within us. It is intended as a guide for thinking about happiness in the context of mystical Jewish wisdom. It is not a recipe for instant gratification, nor is it a scholarly text. It doesn't offer potions for dissolving the challenges that accompany everyone's journey through life. What it does provide is a step-by-step understanding of how we make ourselves miserable and of time-honored spiritual approaches for thinking and living that can extricate us from that less-than-desirable state.

Finding Joy is designed to be accessible to readers of all faiths who are eager to draw on the wisdom of Jewish mysticism. In order to make it accessible, I had to make this a creative interpretation of the traditional Kabbalah. It can enlighten anyone curious about Jewish spirituality. But most of all, *Finding Joy* is for:

- People who have never been happy. Here, they might discover a unique path to happiness that finally works.
- People who once had happiness, but lost it. Here, they will find strategies for a second chance at enjoying life fully.
- People who have suffered personal loss or tragedy. Doctors say that once a broken bone heals, it is strongest at the point of the break. Readers coping with emotional traumas might here discover a therapeutic process that will make them stronger than before.

The idea for *Finding Joy* came from a class on Jewish mysticism that I taught several years ago to adults at Temple Shir Shalom in West Bloomfield, Michigan. Some students told me that, while the course had been an interesting exploration of theory, it had not given them any ideas about how mystical thought could be applied to *real* problems. Instead of just historical information, arcane formulas or facts once hidden in ancient texts, these adults wanted lessons for life.

I reshaped the course I taught the next year to incorporate the premise that happiness and spirituality were linked. Enrollment for this new class doubled from that of the previous year, and attendance at each class kept increasing. By the end of the course, more than 100 people were showing up; about a third were not Jewish. Many said they had been attracted by the distillation of the mystical material into easy-to-manage ideas. By combining metaphors, stories and case histories with mystical principles, the students gained an insight into the world of *Kabbalah.*

Kabbalah, which literally means "receiving," is the generic term frequently used for Jewish mysticism. Practitioners of Kabbalah wanted to convince utterly rational people that the world is filled with mystery and utterly irrational events. Believing is seeing, they might say. Centuries before the science of psychology was born, the Kabbalists examined depression and manic joy, creating blueprints and formulas to heal the wounded heart or cure the sickly soul.

None of what the Kabbalists crafted is really counter to modern psychology or science. A recent study of 30,000 Americans over the age of 100, for example, found that the secret to long life was more spiritual than physical. Scientists discovered that diet, exercise and healthy living, while contributing to a good life, were not the prime factors behind the longevity of these centenarians. What, then, was the potion for an extended stay on this earth? Coping successfully with loss, keeping busy, and maintaining a positive attitude.

The difficulty with Kabbalah, as any student of Jewish mysticism knows, is that it can be dense and seem quite disconnected from modern life. With the collaboration of Mark Hass, a journalist and former newspaper editor, I set out to overcome that problem. When my ideas met his skepticism and need for clarity, a practical and accessible form of spirituality was born that is the foundation for this book. He gave a voice to my notion that spirituality isn't something just to be studied, but rather that it can be a pragmatic and functional tool for making our lives more pleasurable.

That's why this is a book that you, the reader, should feel free to use in whatever way makes sense to you. Read the case studies, all of which are the real stories of real people whose names I've changed, and look for ways that they parallel your own. Read the "Exercises for the Soul" that conclude each chapter. These concisely list things you can do to bring yourself closer to a spiritual happiness. Incorporate them into your daily routine. Read the text from beginning to end, or study a single chapter that has special meaning to you, and return to other parts of the book later.

Regardless of how you tailor this information to your needs, it is my hope and Mark's that when you're done, you will feel inspired by Jewish mysticism. It will be the essential measure of our success if, after reading this book, you are comfortable enough with the ideas of practical spirituality to talk about them with others and to incorporate them into your life. If you can do so, you will be closer to achieving a happiness within, and you will be closer to finding joy in your everyday life and throughout your days.

CHAPTER I

WHY DIDN'T YOU ENJOY ALL THE PERMITTED PLEASURES?

Happiness wasn't something that just happened to Molly. Most of the people who know her would say just the opposite: That her past seven years had been filled with the kind of tragedy that would cripple the best of us and drive the rest close to mental or physical collapse.

Molly's 24-year-old daughter died of a previously undiscovered congenital heart problem just two years before her husband was diagnosed with a deadly form of cancer. There was never even time to grieve properly, to relieve herself gradually of the burden of her child's death, to make herself whole. Her transition from mother of a dying child to wife of a dying man was nearly seamless.

Her husband died after three years of painful illness. Even though Molly knew his death was coming, even though they had talked about her life without him and how it would be when he passed from her, she was not prepared. The medical bills had exhausted their savings, the emotional roller

19

coaster had sapped her strength. She felt immobilized, lost. But, only for a while.

I saw Molly fourteen months after her husband's death. She was on an outing at a professional baseball game with some coworkers. Molly had found a job to make ends meet. She had rediscovered something else: Joy. She was interacting with everyone around her enthusiastically, as if she had not been touched by pain. She was having fun, and that's why she'd organized this visit to the ballpark, even though she wasn't much of a baseball fan. Doing it gave her purpose: To make herself happy and make others happy in the process.

As I got to know this new Molly in the following months, I would realize that was the key to her happiness. By working at being happy, she had emerged from what could have been a life of anger, powerlessness and sadness. Sure, she'd taken classes on how to cope with grief, read the usual books, listened to the advice of family and friends, and probably learned something from all of that. But her personal commitment to finding happiness and her willingness to work at it gave her a structure for pursuing a joyful life.

"I started by practicing the little things," she said. "If being alone was getting me down, I realized that I had to be with other people. But being with other people was difficult. So I practiced. I would get dressed up every morning, even though I had no place to go. By the time I realized the emptiness that surrounded me, the sympathy calls had stopped and people rarely called. So I called old friends. But they had husbands; they didn't have my hurt. So I chose people I knew would understand if I cried every now and then, or if I fell quiet during a conversation. These people were in similar situations to mine or were people I'd known a long time.

"It was difficult when I started, but that's what practicing is all about. At first, I practiced going to the movies with people. Before the movie, I talked about what we were going to see. After the movie, I talked about what we'd seen. After mastering that, I started practicing going to dinner with people, and then I practiced *really* talking with them. Then I got into a groove and out of my rut. Now, a day doesn't go by that I don't practice some aspect of living."

Pursuing a Clearheaded Spirituality

Those who say that Molly had repressed her true feelings would be wrong. In fact, Molly's approach is clearheaded and spiritual. It is consistent with teachings in the fundamental texts of Jewish mysticism, which hold remarkable insights for Jews and non-Jews alike who are searching for a happiness that seems to elude them.

The texts of the Kabbalah, the *Zohar,* the *Bahir* and the *Sefer Yetzira,* in addition to mystical portions of the more familiar and accessible Talmud, have rarely been used to shape a practical conceptual basis for making life happier. That's a shame, because the mystics have some good advice about happiness. The Jewish mystical tradition is centered on the belief that with a spiritual focus, joy is possible and greater appreciation of the world is achievable, no matter what our problems or pain may be. Making life more fulfilling and enjoyable, then, is the basis of any spiritual formula for living.

Mystics understood the simple truth of human existence: Happiness is to be treasured and welcomed into every life. The key to this thinking is found in the Talmud, which tells us that upon death every person will be asked the following questions to determine their eternal fate:

Were you honest in business?

Did you set aside time for study?

Did you have hope?

Did you enjoy all the permitted pleasures of life? Or, why weren't you happy with those pleasures you did experience?

For many of us, the problem is as simple as not understanding what true happiness is and not recognizing that the cloth of contentment and joy are woven with the threads of spirituality. Happiness results from a frequency of positive emotions and a minimizing of life's pain. It is the sum total of all the positive emotions we can muster. By concentrating on the positive, we can create happiness which can help put the painful, problematic parts of our lives into perspective.

How Helpful Is Self-Help?

Several years ago, I met a woman very different than Molly. Janet was a successful lawyer, married to a handsome and successful man who adored her. She had two bright, healthy children. Her thirty-one years of life had been unmarked by disease, failure or tragedy of any kind. Not even a distant relative had died.

Still, she worries. She worries a lot. She worries that,

despite being a partner at a major law firm in a large Midwestern city, perhaps she is not truly successful. "If I were in New York or Los Angeles," she says a bit arrogantly, "I could be really big, maybe a national figure." She worries about the car she drives, a top-of-the-line Mercedes, because it squeaks when she makes right turns, and its color shows road dirt, and one of her partners has a Porsche that seems to make more of a statement. She likes being married, but thinks other young couples are more respected or liked. She loves her children, but worries that her friends' children are reading better than her own.

"Sure, I've made it," she says. "But I feel that I should be happier. Why can't I be happy?"

To answer that question, she became an avid user of self-help books and tapes. She passed, like many, through a series of fads based on Eastern religions. She tried countless diets to take off those last stubborn few pounds from her lithe athletic body, thinking that happiness is a physical state that she could achieve after a day of eating carrots and running a treadmill. She tried hobbies, a psychotherapist and, finally, pills to alter her mood. But one afternoon, she appeared at my office totally despondent.

"Maybe," she hoped, "you can find something in my soul that will make me happy."

I began by telling her about a professor I had in college who, at the first class in each semester of his beginning-level psychology course, before even introducing himself or telling his students what they'd learn, would draw a large dot in the center of a sheet of white paper. He then held the paper over his head and asked his curious students: "What do you see?"

Dozens of answers came from every corner of the lecture hall. Many of the professor's more clever students who thought the dot was a Rorschach test let their minds wander: A butterfly, the earth, the tip of a very red rose. Others were more literal. They saw a black dot or a maybe a black dot with tiny white specks in it.

When the students became quiet, the professor lowered the drawing, looked at it as if he were trying to assess each answer he'd received, and said: "I see a sheet of paper with a dot in its center, eight and a half by eleven inches with a spot that perhaps covers twenty percent of the total writing surface available on this one side. I could write the Declaration of Independence, the Magna Carta, the entire Bill of Rights on this one sheet of paper. Yet, all you saw was the black dot."

He paused, allowing his point to penetrate. Then he drove that point home: "That is how most people view their lives. Let that be your first lesson in psychology."

My professor's point is that most of us are so busy studying the black dots that mar our lives that we lose sight of the bold whiteness of possibility that surrounds those dots. We don't see our accomplishments and how we touched the world in a positive way because of those insignificant dots, the problems, the troubles large and small over which we have no control. We just know we'll never be happy. And, if we're not happy something must be wrong.

Happiness Comes with the Right Attitude
under Any Circumstance

We don't partake of what the Talmud calls "the permissible pleasures," because we let the black spots block our view. Minimizing those obstacles and maximizing the possibilities that surround them is the goal of practical spirituality.

It's not that easy, though. Even mystics and spiritual people throughout history realized that the world conspires to make the average person unhappy. It is not a plot devised by some evil genie or a cosmic joke or a test created by a divinity eager to grade us on our grace under pressure. Things happen, pain happens, problems happen, sometimes for no apparent reason. There are times when we will be exposed to the worst that life has to offer. Even barring that, none of us is immune from the scrapes and crises of everyday life, no matter how rich or well-known we may be. The fancy new car *will* squeak. It *will* get dirty. It might even break down.

The black dot that makes a day miserable is frequently a small problem. A tiny hole in an otherwise unconsidered tooth. Thousands of our body parts may be working perfectly, but one small sprain of an obscure tendon and our well-exercised machine can become an utter wreck that seems to demand our full attention and energy. Once we're miserable, we seek out like company and spread gloom to others.

Think of all the ways a day can be ruined in the first hour after awakening. The toast can burn; the milk can be sour. Your spouse can be a bit surly. The school bus may come too early or your child may get out the door too late.

Good mornings are hard to come by if you let the pain of living get you down.

Jewish mystics teach that a happy person is not someone who has just the right set of circumstances. Instead, the happy person is someone who has the right attitude about any circumstance and is able to communicate that attitude to his or her soul, and then do something either to heighten a positive experience or lessen a negative one. It is crucial, mystics say, to realize that the sharpest stones beneath our bare feet can be diamonds, if we just recognize them as such. In other words, a happy person can bounce back from failure or defeat not only by looking at the bright side, but also by learning from the dark side.

Remember that Albert Einstein flunked math in grade school. Edgar Allan Poe and Salvador Dali were expelled from college. Thomas Edison was at the bottom of his class. Every genius and every true talent has a way of finally blossoming.

Then there was Abraham Lincoln, whose entire life was a series of rebounds from adversity. He failed in business at the age of 22; ran for the Illinois state legislature and lost at age 23; failed again at business at 24; ran again for the legislature and was elected at age 25. His sweetheart died when he was 26. He suffered an emotional breakdown at 27. He was defeated in a bid to be the Speaker of the Illinois House of Representatives at age 29 and lost a run for the U.S. Congress at 39. After achieving that goal a short time later, he ran for U.S. Senate and lost at age 46. At age 51, he won the nation's highest office.

Learn to Recite Blessings over the Ordinary

For most of us though, happiness is less a matter of bouncing back from defeat than making the routine parts of our lives seem interesting. It is so easy for us to go through day-to-day on cruise control, with our senses and minds disconnected. The mystics tell us that when we put ourselves on automatic we are merely going through the motions of life and not consciously noticing what's around us. This tendency to cruise is our answer to daily routine. At best, it is a meaningless rest period that helps us get through the more mundane parts of our day. At worst, it is dangerous, physically and spiritually.

Insurance statistics show that most automobile accidents occur close to home. One of the reasons? Our senses are dulled by the routine, and we lose focus. We daydream. We don't see that car stopped at the red light. Think about how often we enter that catatonic-like state. Reading a book, we may suddenly realize we've turned the last several pages without a clue about what we've read. Or we may misplace our keys or our wallet and have no idea where we left them.

When this happens, we are in what psychiatrists call the "trance of ordinary life," missing life's many opportunities for growth, learning and development. Consider the tale of David Rice Atchison, who could have briefly been president of the United States. His moment in history arrived when president-elect Zachary Taylor made a decision based on his faith in 1850. Taylor refused to be inaugurated on Sunday, March 4, because it was the Christian Sabbath. By moving the inauguration to the next day, the nation had no elected chief executive for 24 hours because Taylor's predecessor, President James Polk, left office as scheduled at Sunday noon. The rules of succession left a U.S. Senator named Atchison in line to become president, at least for a day.

Unfortunately, Atchison, a man who enjoyed a good party and a good many drinks, was out late the night before making the rounds of the inauguration celebrations. Before passing out, he left specific instructions not to be disturbed all day on Sunday. By the time he opened his eyes and stretched and yawned on Monday afternoon, he'd literally slept through his entire "term" as president.

These diversions that grab our attention when we go through life automatically, like a good party and a good drink, are the equivalent of my professor's black dot. They are all we see. For many of us, these are always about pain, discomfort and the sleep of everyday life. We must practice avoiding them if we ever hope to be truly happy.

Consider this story about a man named Mordechai, whom I met several years ago in Israel near the Western Wall. I was talking in English to a group of people, and he stopped nearby to listen. When I finished my impromptu lecture on the history and theological meaning of the Wall, Mordechai tapped me on the shoulder, and, in the softest voice, asked where I was from. When I told him, a glowing smile spread across his face. His uncle came from the same place. He asked me to recite the traditional Jewish blessing that marked coincidence. When I did, he said, "Amen."

When I told him I was a rabbi leading a tour of the Holy Land, that smile returned, and he informed me that this was his lucky day. To meet a rabbi from the same place as his uncle was so fortunate that he felt compelled to recite the blessing spoken upon meeting a scholar. And I, of course, said, "Amen." After I answered each question from Mordechai, he found a reason to marvel. Something about each answer was utterly wonderful and amazing to him. He responded with a blessing, and I with an amen.

When I ran into Mordechai several days later, I asked him about all those blessings. "I make it a practice to meet many interesting people from all over the world," he said. "You see, I believe that God records every blessing that every one of us ever speaks. All God has to do is count how many blessings I've said and how many times I've made others realize the coincidental blessings in their lives. In this way, I can't miss being with the Holy One for eternity.

"You see, my rabbi," he continued with reverence and that wonderful smile, "the one with the most 'amens' in the end, wins."

Mordechai was able to see the blessings all around him. In turn, he was able to extend the boundaries of what is sacred and understand that the real purpose of life is to work at achieving happiness, to practice seeing the "permitted pleasures" of life.

If we let our senses be dulled by the mundane, we will lose the resiliency of our spirit. If we don't exercise our inner joy, we will not be able to cope with the worst of times, nor appreciate the joy from the best of times.

Joy Must Be Practiced

The mystics advise a simple strategy to avoid "losing it."

Because holiness, they say, is wrapped in very ordinary clothing, we just need to be focused enough to see what's special in the familiar things around us. Like muscles that have to be used to avoid atrophy, the soul must be constantly aware and interact with the physical side of life or it will lose its ability to buoy us when we are down or temper our emotions when we are up. This strategy is what the mystics call the daily exercise of the soul: Practice.

So, like an athlete, we practice, but still we're troubled. What is the goal of our practice? When do we know whether we've succeeded?

Jewish tradition gives us a goal: We should say one hundred blessings each day. When we try it, we discover that it's quite difficult to find one hundred things each day for which to be thankful. So difficult, in fact, that we spend most of our time looking.

In the course of looking, we find many things worth noting that might have otherwise passed us by. That's the goal. The practiced eye sees far more than the lazy one. As a result, the more we look for happiness, the more we can see it. Happiness then becomes not a final state to be achieved, but a process, a way of life and of living it in a spiritual way. It's something that we can do day in and day out.

This process of searching for one hundred blessings also creates an important awareness: That it is impossible to be happy all the time. We may never reach one hundred blessings, but there's still plenty to be happy about. Many things bring us joy, no matter what our struggles or misfortunes.

There's a wonderful story, popularized by the writer Robert Fulghum, about a man who felt discouraged because he was only happy half the time. He went to his rabbi in tears, moaning that he felt like a failure. The rabbi stroked his beard (all rabbis in stories seem to have beards), nodded his head wisely and suggested cryptically that the man refer to a specific page of the current *World Almanac of Facts.*

The surprised fellow dutifully followed the rabbi's instruction and came back, confused. "I don't understand," said the troubled man, showing the rabbi the book. "All I can find on that page is a list of baseball batting statistics."

The rabbi pointed at a line on the page. The man read it aloud: "Highest lifetime batting averages."

"And who is at the top of that list?" the rabbi asked.

The man answered: "Ty Cobb, with a lifetime average of .367."

The rabbi looked deeply into the man's disconsolate eyes and said: "So?"

The man was disturbed. "I don't understand," he said.

"Listen, my friend," the rabbi answered. "Ty Cobb only got a base hit once every three times, but still he was the best, still he made the Hall of Fame."

The man, in despair, twisted his hands together anxiously. "I'm not a baseball fan," he said. "I don't understand."

The rabbi rose from behind his desk, frustrated. "If one out of three got Ty Cobb into the Hall of Fame, then you are a superstar, because you told me you were happy one of every two days," the rabbi said. "You're batting .500. So don't complain."

What the rabbi didn't say is that, with a little practice, who knows what heights the man might have reached. With a little practice, when asked that fateful question upon his death, "Why didn't you enjoy all the permitted pleasures?" he could answer, "But I did."

Exercises for the Soul

Monday   Look for opportunities to say "Thank you." Each time you say it, you will make two people happy. One of the major concepts of prayer is the expression of gratitude. When you say "Thank you," even to God, you show that you recognize and appreciate the gift that you've been given.

Tuesday   Be alone for twenty minutes near the end of the day. No television, no radio, no books, no newspapers. Commuting to and from work doesn't count. Just sit alone in a quiet place and think of the good things from your day. Reflect. Don't plan ahead. Savor the moment.

Wednesday   Buy or pick a single flower. Choose the most beautiful or the most fragrant. Take the flower home. Note its uniqueness. Treasure the reason you selected it. Now appreciate one aspect of yourself or of someone close to you that is special, unique and beautiful.

Thursday   Apologize to someone you love. Do it the hard way. If it feels uncomfortable to write a letter, write one.

If a personal apology would cause you the most distress, that's what you do. An apology is an act of clarity. It focuses us on the relationship between our actions and the feelings of others.

Friday
Treat yourself to a food you truly enjoy. Recite a blessing (any blessing that you choose) over it, before or after eating.

Saturday
Say something praiseworthy to someone. Say it so not only that person can hear it, but so others can, as well.

Sunday
Do something special by yourself that you wouldn't normally do, but that you enjoy. Go see a specific painting at the museum or a certain animal you are curious about at the zoo or attend a concert at the symphony hall.

CHAPTER 2

MIND OVER MATTER:

IF YOU DON'T MIND, IT DOESN'T MATTER

At the corners of the Medieval world, there was a big dragon that would do unspeakable things to any sailor foolish enough to travel near. One foolish sailor heard the common wisdom: Don't go there. But he also heard another voice: Find out for yourself. He was, the Jewish mystics would say, in the hands of his dueling *Yetzer*, inner predisposition's struggling to control his actions.

This chapter is about that struggle and how it shapes our ability to find happiness. It's not so much about good and evil or lightness and dark, but rather about the dual nature of the human soul. We need both pieces, the positive and the negative, to be complete, but we need also to recognize how they tug back and forth for control of our lives. By understanding that process, we have the potential to influence it.

The positive predisposition, the *Yetzer Hatov*, kept telling the medieval sailor to invest the effort in finding the truth and whatever else he'd discover along the way. Set your own course, it said. The negative predisposition, the *Yetzer Hara*, argued passionately against taking risk: Everyone knew what was out there, and everyone was scared.

In his thoughtful book, *A Kick in the Seat of the Pants*, philosopher Roger Von Oech told how those dragons came about. When the map makers ran out of what was known about the world before they ran out of parchment, they would sketch a dragon at the edge of the scroll.

This was a sign to sailors that they would be approaching territory that was totally unknown, a symbol that they were going into uncharted waters. The dragons were merely design elements, nothing more, which could easily be drawn as large or as small as was needed to fill the space available.

As it is with everything in life, many people took the symbol literally and believed that someone must have seen sea monsters. They were on the map, so they must exist. For these people, the *Yetzer Hara* held sway. They were all too willing to accept unquestioningly the fears and the views of other people whom they trusted or whom they assumed knew what they seemed to know.

Learn to Trust Yourself

How often in our own lives do we take the same course, the easy way, the path that allows us to rely on others, the experts who we assume know everything? Why are we willing to depend on these experts, who frequently fall victim to the same *Yetzer Hara* and take the road that requires less of them?

Consider:

When Charles H. Duel became the commissioner of the United States Patent Office in 1899, he asked President William McKinley to abolish his office. "Everything that can be invented has been invented!" he said.

In 1865, Joshua Coopersmith was arrested for fraud because he was trying to raise funds to work on something he called "the telephone." An editorial in the *Boston Post* complimented the wisdom of the arrest. "Well informed people know it is impossible to transmit the voice over wires," stated the *Post*. "And that, were it possible to do so, the thing would be of no practical value."

In 1943, the chairman of IBM, Thomas J. Watson, told friends: "I think there is a world market for about five computers."

The president of Digital Equipment Corporation told a group of experts in 1977, "There is no reason for any individual to have a computer in their home."

It is always easier to go with what is not possible than what is. It is in our nature not to take risks or explore the world or search for the shape of the future. This is the *Yetzer Hara*, the negative inclination that doesn't demand thought and doesn't want to see things through to their end.

This is the inclination that drives us toward immediate gratification and impatience. The *Yetzer Hatov*, on the other hand, might have led Digital's president in 1977 to the same conclusion reached at the time by the people running Apple and other small computer companies that eventually grew into giants. If only he had listened to the inclination inside him that said the future was not yet determined: Figure it out; don't just reject it. "Turn it over and over again," as the Talmud teaches. If Digital's CEO had done that, I might be writing these words on a Digital desktop computer...and its corporate president might be a legend.

The doctrine of these two drives is a major component of Jewish psychology. It personifies the duality of choice between good and evil. Instead of the Greek or Roman gods battling with each other for a human soul, the human has two opposing tendencies constantly tugging and pushing him or her. Talmudic scholars believed the *Yetzer Hara* was an almost overwhelming passion, an uncontrollable appetite comparable to sexual lust. Untamed, this would lead to disastrous consequences: Rage, jealousy, even rape and murder.

But without it, a human being would have no desire to do anything. It was understood that the desire that leads to healthy sexual encounters, also leads to love, marriage and children. The *Yetzer Hara* is only dangerous when it's uncontrolled.

God Is Present When We Positively React to Problems

Buddhists believe that the source of all pain is unfulfilled desire and unmet expectations. Their strategy to avoid pain is to avoid expectation and desire. Of course, there is then a price to pay: If you were to take this concept to its logical extreme no progress, no advancement, no secular improvement would ever be necessary. Without risk, there can be none of those things. Jewish philosophical teachings recognize that desire and expectation are part of the life process and can be healthy if they are controlled and moderated.

According to the biblical commentaries, the *Yetzer Hara* is part of a person's makeup from birth. Jewish rabbinical thought suggests that the *Yetzer Hatov*, a positive inclination that centers on the intellect and a conscious effort to remain balanced, is not normally present or relevant until puberty. That's when an individual has the ability to reason and understand.

It is believed that when we become old enough to reflect, we realize that God is not in someone's cancer or in a hurricane or in evil. God is present in people's positive reactions to the pain and problems that make life seem unendurable. God is there when we use our most positive side to help, to create, to make ourselves or someone else whole or happy. The *Yetzer Hatov* is always present. It just needs to be used in order to be felt, and this will make the presence of God felt, as well.

The problem with all of this is that the dark side is seemingly more powerful because it is filled with passion and emotion. In the context of the Talmud, it is like a stranger who, invited into a home as a guest, ends up making himself master of the house.

No one is immune from the power of the *Yetzer Hara*, from its anger, vindictiveness, vanity and greed. Our accomplishments, our intelligence, our personal power and influence don't protect us. In fact, the rabbis believe that the greater the person, the stronger and more evident his dark side. Perhaps this is so because powerful people do not believe they will be caught, or feel they deserve a few perks, or just assume that they are so good they can do no wrong, or they shouldn't be critically judged for the wrong they do.

Was that what happened to a once-prominent New York State chief judge who was sentenced to a prison term for threatening to kidnap the daughter of his former lover? The bizarre, highly publicized saga of Judge Sol Wachtler is a chilling example of how the powerful can be destroyed by their own sense of immunity.

Wachtler, Chief Judge of the New York Court of Appeals and frequently mentioned as a gubernatorial candidate, was at the peak of his public stature in 1993 when something went wrong. Following the breakup of a love affair with a prominent New York socialite and Republican fundraiser, Wachtler, a married man with children and a promising future, sent obscene extortion letters to his former mistress.

After he was caught, he denied writing the letters. Then he blamed his former lover for driving him to commit his bizarre acts. Finally, he blamed a mental illness, which had been made worse by an explosive mixture of amphetamines and tranquilizers.

Wachtler's defense was essentially that some force beyond his control had made him act irrationally: The devil made him do it. Indeed, in the Talmudic tradition, the *Yetzer Hara* is personified by Satanic influence. The belief is that the devil *can* make you do it, no matter how far you've come, how impressive your achievements, how substantial your wealth or goodness.

That is why it is easier to listen to that negative inclination. It's easier to react emotionally to events in our lives, rather than to respond thoughtfully to them. It is easy to get upset because the newspaper didn't arrive on time or the toast burns, and then let these things ruin our day.

But it is more challenging to deal with events thought-fully and positively, to make a mental note to buy a newspaper at the newsstand or to toast another piece of bread and try out the new jam that might make the inconvenience worth-while. It is more demanding to put things in their proper perspective. An undelivered newspaper, after all, is not dis-ease, destruction or death. How many of us react as if it were, only because we aren't willing to make the effort re-quired by our *Yetzer Hatov*?

Take Control of Your Thoughts

If we continue to look at ways that the *Yetzer Hara* shapes our lives, we realize that a multitude of our personal short-comings grow from the soil of this negative inclination.

Most of us, for example, suffer from the disease of low expectations. We fear failure. When his work was slow on the Sistine Chapel, Michelangelo told Pope Julius II, "I told you that I was no painter." When we read the Gettysburg Address, we see Abraham Lincoln's nagging doubts about the value of his words when he writes: "The world will little note, nor long remember, what we say here."

Few of us have a natural ability to think positively. Few have a soul in which the *Yetzer Hatov* dominates, in which the positive inclination occupies what a computer program might refer to as the default mode.

How many people wake up each morning with a smile on their faces? How many feel good no matter what hap-pens? How many are convinced that wherever they are is the best place on earth, that they lead a charmed life and that the people who love them are the most wonderful people in the world?

As small a group as that is, think of how many fewer people there are who never had to study for tests, who seemed to breeze through high school, college and professional schools, who seemed to have it made? How rare the natural athletes, who were able to hit a baseball or sink baskets effortlessly or ski or ice skate so well that the rest of us paled in comparison.

Finally, how many truly gifted people are out there? How many were born prodigies? How many can be like Toscanini, who had perfect pitch throughout his life, or Mozart, who could play any tune he heard by the time he was three years old? Who among us can match the innate tennis skills of Chris Evert?

The overwhelming majority of us are neither naturally happy nor born with spectacular gifts. We are all, indeed, fertile ground for the *Yetzer Hara*. We emerge from the womb crying that the world is not fair. As children, we expected our parents, who had the nerve to give us life, to take care of our every whim. We were out of town when perfect musical pitch was passed around or we clumsily slipped during our dance recital. Or won the "Most Improved Camper Award," the one reserved for the person who couldn't win anything else. It is so difficult for most of us just to get through our childhood that we grow accustomed to feeling that life is really very unfair.

The mystics believe that negative thinking poisons the soul and creates unhappiness. Because negative thoughts, even though destructive, arc easier to believe than positive ones, they become the path of least resistance. They are our default mode, our automatic setting, and it eventually becomes natural to assume the worst. We are predisposed to look at the glass half empty because, throughout childhood, we learned from our *Yetzer Hara* to expect failure, to fear first and ask questions later.

What we need to do is shut off the automatic setting. Kabbalistic thought is based on the realization that life is neither fair or unfair. If we adopt its tenets, we can level the playing field by focusing and taking control of our thoughts.

To understand the origins of our ability to focus, we must understand the mystical notion of *Sefirot,* or rays of light. The Kabbalists believed that before the world was created, perfection existed. God's divine presence was made up of ten rays, or *Sefirot.* When the world was created, the rays were obscured, but they still exist.

The rays permit us to see past imperfections, pain, anger and problems. They light up our world and give us direction and a second sight, which stops us from simply reacting to things as they occur. They help us understand that we don't need immediate gratification.

The *Sefirot* are a bridge to the center of our soul. The highest and most powerful of the rays is the crown, or *Keter,* which shows the way to true happiness, has the ability to help us rise above pettiness and can create goodness, dignity and depth.

Directly below the crown are wisdom, or *Hokhmah,* and understanding, or *Binah.* These correspond to active, receptive intelligence.

The next grouping of rays includes mercy, or *Chesed;*

beauty, or *Tiferet*; and strength, or *Gevurah*. These three create a balance with strength and mercy on opposite sides, and beauty and its ability to bring us inner harmony in the center.

The final grouping of rays is splendor which some believe comes with persistence, or *Hod* on the left. The foundation of all, which some feel is our attitude, or *Yesod*, is in the middle. The natural outcome of persistence and attitude is victory, *Netzah*, on the right.

Finally, the lowest of the *Sefirot* is *Malkhut*, which translates into English as "kingdom," but can be more clearly thought of as "success."

Even Einstein Was "Albert" to His Teacher

The mystics believed that each of these rays helps us understand and appreciate the divine forces within us. When we realize that we don't have the intelligence of an Einstein, we should also try to remember that, when Einstein was just "Albert" to his teachers, he wasn't considered that smart, either. When conductor/composer Leonard Bernstein's father was asked what it was like to have a musical genius for a son, his answer was, "At the time, I didn't know my Leonard was going to be *the* Leonard Bernstein!"

And even if we're not born with exquisite talent, the power of the *Sefirot* and our *Yetzer Hatov* can help us to achieve far more than the person who has natural ability and to be happier than the person seemingly born that way. Consider this story of two brothers:

Jon, a straight-A student, coasted through high school.

He would brag that everything came naturally to him.

His parents would marvel at how little time Jon needed to master his studies. They bragged about his various accomplishments. He even won a state tennis championship, starred in school plays and earned a scholarship to a prestigious private university.

His brother, David, was four years younger and found life much more difficult. Constantly being compared to Jon and coming up short, David spent much time studying, but could manage no better than B's and C's. He was always the last selected by any team for any sport and was barely accepted by a local college.

In college, David still studied hard for his B's and C's. Even though he worked as an announcer at the college radio station, he didn't have a natural voice for radio, so he took courses in speech and diction. With his usual persistence, he worked his way up the ladder, making friends along the way. Finally, his hard work and his many friends helped David become the lead sportscaster for his station.

He enjoyed his first real success so much that he wanted more. A teacher suggested he intern at a local television station. Soon after he graduated, the station hired him, first as a production assistant, then as an assistant producer and finally as a producer.

In those days, David told his friends: "I'm not the sharpest tool in the shed, but I know I can be the best. All you have to do is give me time, and all I have to do is work at it." In ten years, David become one of the highest paid and most successful sports announcers in the country.

Meanwhile, his brother Jon thought he could breeze

through college as he had through high school. But after losing his scholarship because of poor grades, Jon was asked to leave his prestigious university. He enrolled in another college, became bored and left. He told his parents, "This is just a second-rate school. What can they teach me that I don't already know?"

Jon decided that he didn't need a college degree to go into marketing, so he started selling shoes. When he decided shoes were too dull, he sold men's suits. Then he sold tools. All these jobs went nowhere.

Jon takes his joy now not from accomplishment, but from reliving the old days, while David gets his joy from his success.

Every Crisis Is an Opportunity

The mystics understand that a person's skill may not be born within him. It has to be made. There are times that one just has to accept what the Talmud teaches: Life is neither fair nor unfair; it is time and space that we have to fill with the best we can give, the best we can be.

And even if we don't grow to be a star athlete, a prima ballerina, a world-class surgeon, or a famed painter, we will be able to define our success by how well we match what we love with what we do.

A lover of art need not be Picasso to write about art, teach art, or own a gallery or a framing shop. Ball players who love to play can do so, even if it isn't in the major leagues. We can all find countless things that keep us close to our passions.

I know a lovely man who was crazy about tennis, but he was an average player who never got much better no matter how long he practiced. Yet, he loved everything connected with the sport, and he hated his job as an insurance salesman. He read all the tennis magazines and every book about the sport.

When someone told him about a small shop that would soon close, making a rental space available, he convinced a few manufacturers of tennis equipment to sell him their seconds and returns on consignment. He took over the store's lease and worked in the shop on weekends, advertising his extensive discounts.

People came into the store not just to buy equipment, but to pick his brain about tennis. His shop now occupies one quarter of a large strip mall. No longer selling insurance, he now runs a thriving business that lets him do exactly what he loves.

What he did was create an opportunity with his *Yetzer Hatov*. He didn't complain about how miserable he was as an insurance salesman; he thought of a way to remake his life so it would bring him happiness.

No matter the obstacle, it is possible for all of us to create an opportunity by relying on our *Yetzer Hatov*. The Kabbalists believed that every crisis was an opportunity to use our soul as leverage against all of life's little pains and problems, to strengthen it for the big pains and problems that you will face.

The Talmudic thinkers taught: "Don't pray for a lighter load. Pray instead for a stronger back."

That is a cross-cultural idea. The Chinese character for

"crisis" is the same as the one used for "opportunity."

By thinking of each crisis as an opportunity, we can figure out ways to turn apparent burdens into assets. Doing so is a victory for the *Yetzer Hatov*.

Positive Thoughts Make Positive Souls

The foundation of a spiritual basis for happiness is realizing that no one is born with everything and no one is lucky all the time. Even the most gifted people probably wish that they could also do something else equally well. Einstein may have wished he could be a soccer star; maybe Toscanini dreamed of being a better public speaker.

No matter how much or how little we are blessed, one thing is certain: Concentrating on what's wrong will never make us whole. Before we can experience happiness, we have to focus on the positive aspect of every situation. Doing so will create a positive soul within, and that will shape our lives outside.

Consider the story of Gene Mitchner. As a child, he contracted a rare illness that left him crippled and in a wheelchair. During his school years, his classmates would tease him. In return, he would try to find a humorous response and managed to change their ridicule into acceptance.

When he graduated from high school, perhaps because of his popularity, people in his town offered to set Gene up in a business running a popcorn stand in the town square. Gene was thankful, but believed that they were putting limits on what he might achieve.

After graduation, he worked with some friends who had

formed a rock-and-roll band. At a San Diego nightclub, the band was having technical problems and couldn't get its show started. One band member asked him distract the audience until the band was ready to play.

Gene made some jokes about himself and his wheelchair. In the process, he launched a successful career in comedy. Twenty years after his friends expected that he could run a popcorn stand and do little more, Gene Mitchner came home a hero: The most successful graduate of his class and the grand marshal of the homecoming parade.

"If you're complaining about what life has dealt you," he said that day, "go out and pick up your own set of cards and deal again."

Exercises for the Soul

Monday   Think of two positive attributes with which you were born and how you can use them to your advantage today.

Tuesday   Think of two successes you've had in your life and try to understand how they shaped who you are today.

Wednesday   Conquer a fear. If you have been avoiding a potentially unpleasant phone conversation, make the call and get past it.

Thursday	Turn a negative into a positive. For example, place an audio tape that you especially like in your car, so that if you get stuck in traffic you can listen and enjoy it while you wait. Or, carry a magazine that you like to read in your briefcase, so that if you get stuck waiting for someone you can spend the time in a satisfying way.
Friday	Call someone you like. During the conversation, tell them why you admire them.
Saturday	Close your eyes. Recall and feel the joy of doing something that you love.
Sunday	Reward yourself. Do something for an hour that you really want to do.

CHAPTER 3

THE BATTLE FOR OUR MINDS

A sow's ear into a silk purse. Chicken soup from chicken feathers.

The notion that we can turn misfortune into advantage resounds throughout the folk lore and folk psychology of many people, and with good reason. The notion is true.

Think about it. We all know someone who made good, and whose success seemed unexpected. Those voted least likely to succeed in high school can return to a twenty-fifth class reunion driving the biggest car or wearing the biggest smile.

Paradoxically, we also know those who were blessed with every advantage, yet managed to trample and tear the silk purse they were handed.

What separates these two groups? What secrets let us leverage what God has given us into happiness?

Jewish mysticism offers some clues to this when it reminds us that everyone has a *Yetzer Hara* that can create bad habits, inner pain, addictions or co-dependencies. They can also be what makes us unique, powerful, successful and happy.

Consider Alan and what he calls his "inner dragon." This fire-breather is no Disney character, no Saturday morning cartoon. It is a germ that might have poisoned his soul long ago, a justifiable anger that we all could understand. It could have easily led him to drug or alcohol abuse, violence or other self-destructive paths. Then, we would have watched Alan when he went on a tabloid TV talk show and explained his failed life.

Alan readily admits that he is angry at his long-dead father for repeatedly beating him as a child for small or imagined infractions, for poor grades, or for not sitting still at the dinner table. He is angry at his aged mother who did not stop his father's attacks. He is angry with his teachers, who attributed his school problems to a learning disability and never had the patience, insight or wisdom to help him.

But, instead of seeing Alan on the more sordid TV shows, we are likely to see him on the evening news speaking as an effective advocate of the legal rights of his clients. As a successful defense attorney, he consciously refuses to let his anger control his life. He makes it work for him the way a fine athlete uses physical skill as a lever for victory, the way a great scientist can build inquisitiveness into a Nobel Prize. Alan believes that his anger is a gift from God because it forces him to fight harder for those who depend on him in court.

"Every time I'm in the public arena, I'm fighting for an eight-year-old child who is getting hit with a wooden hanger," Alan says. "Sometimes I imagine my sixth-grade teacher telling me that, even though I worked hard for the honor of being the class attendance monitor, I couldn't do it because I wasn't smart enough. She was too preoccupied with herself to discover why I was having trouble in school."

Using Your Negativity Productively

Anger is Alan's *Yetzer Hara*. Instead of letting it destroy him, he has channeled it into a tool that makes him more effective, more productive, more successful and more happy.

"I'm actually very lucky," he once said. "I have found the dragon inside me and, instead of slaying it, I put it to work for me. It is with me every day, whether I win or lose in court. It's an advantage that only I have."

Alan has been interviewed by the best that the nation's media can throw at him, and all any viewer, listener or reader can see is that he is a charming, committed, intelligent man defending a cause in which he believes deeply.

Anger. Desire. Passion. These drive human success. The energy from them, properly harnessed, is part of the mystical formula for happiness. But, as with any potent fuel, they can be dangerous.

History is full of examples of a *Yetzer Hara* that first brought great creativity, then led to destruction. Vincent Van Gogh's passions gave birth to great art, but drove him mad. Michelangelo's brilliance obsessed him, but made him and those around him miserable.

There was an amazing couple, Richard and Carol, who created several successful television comedy series. His humor was dark and biting; her writing was exceptional. Richard was convinced that his humor had its roots in his manic depression. Medication would have evened out his highs and lows. Yet, he was sure that if he took medicine that made him better, he would no longer be funny.

Richard was willing to let his *Yetzer Hara* rule his life because he believed his success depended on letting his dark side romp freely through his soul. That success exacted an enormous toll. He lost everything in his life that had value. Richard is lonely and heartbroken. His wife has left him. His children won't see him. Even he hates himself.

But he's rich, and the critics love him. Sitcom producers always take his calls. Richard would have had none of that without his *Yetzer Hara*.

Jewish mystics would say that much of what makes us special can also bring us demons. The battle to create a balance between the *Yetzer Hara* and the *Yetzer Hatov* forces us to grow spiritually. Regulating our *Yetzer Hara* without stifling it makes us unique, deepens our talents and leads to knowledge, which leads to clarity. Clarity gives us control over our *Yetzer Hara* and over our lives. It gives us the inner direction that distinguishes us from every other person and creates a feeling of peace deep within us.

This happiness does not depend on material possessions or pleasure-seeking. Don't believe Madison Avenue and Hollywood that happiness lies in external sources. Money, power, work and sex are overrated in their ability to provide joy. Often, they are empty promises that create problems of their own. As proof, think of how closely related the well-worn deadly sins are to Madison Avenue's efforts to package and sell, to woo, seduce and tantalize.

Even food does little to satisfy our souls. Eating might make us feel better for a while, but too often food becomes a problem itself when we use it to achieve happiness. Who can't recall happy times as a child that were celebrated with cakes and ice-cream sodas? Who doesn't know someone whose poor health was caused by being dependent on food eaten to provide spiritual support? Long before we understood that pharmaceuticals could alter our mood, we learned that food would make us feel better inside, if only for a short time.

And nothing we can buy will bring happiness. In fact, the most miserable people usually aren't those who have suffered catastrophes. The most tormented souls belong to people who had everything they ever wanted—except the power to enjoy it.

Initiative Is Required to Control Negativity

At the Corning Glass factory in upstate New York, a quality-control inspector demonstrates to visitors how this same principle works in glass-making. At a certain point in the glass cooling process, he pours water from a single pitcher into apparently identical goblets standing side-by-side. While most hold the water, one or two shatter. "It's what the glass is made of," he says, "not what you put in it, that counts."

Jewish mystics believe that negative inclinations are driven by our emotions and positive ones are shaped by our intellect. If we follow what seems to be our natural course, the negative inclination will always be dominant, because no thought or initiative will be required. Anything, such as the weather or an inconsiderate driver, can play havoc with our day and make us feel bad.

The writers of the Talmud believed that we had to think constantly about what was happening in our lives if we had any hope of controlling our emotions. Even the simple act of going to sleep or rising from bed demanded thought. When getting into bed, they suggested that we get in on the left side. When leaving the bed, do so on the right. In this way, every day is a complete circle and has unity. That's why when someone is unhappy, short-tempered or in a foul mood, we say he got up on the wrong side of the bed.

These writers were not encouraging us to fixate on rules that seem to have little purpose. Rather, they wanted us to *think* about our lives and take nothing for granted.

A problem can let our *Yetzer Hara* hold sway. Or, it can lead us to focus on finding a solution by using our *Yetzer Hatov*. Witness the widow who has lost everything, but makes her life exciting and rewarding, or the abused child who, as an adult, channels his anger in a positive way, or the man who hates his job, but loves his hobby and eventually makes his hobby his job. Those are all testaments to positive thinking, rather than emotional venting.

Visualization Helps Us Create the Future We Want

The widow, the abused child and the unhappy worker might all say that the first step they took in this process of focused thinking was to visualize what they wanted their lives to be like. Ahead lay much painstaking work to make the vision into reality, but visualization was the indispensable first step. Mind over matter, an idea once scoffed at by scientists, is now in fashion. A growing number of physicians believe it can help our bodies recover from illness. Major corporations have their marketing staffs listen to audio tapes that help them envision higher sales. Athletes are trained to maximize performance by envisioning themselves crossing a finish line. Theodore Herzl, the founder of Zionism, even based a political and philosophical movement on the notion that if we *will* something to happen, it will.

This hard work of visualization is a bit like beginning a journey by pointing ourselves toward our destination before we take a first step. The journey itself is guided by an internal architecture that is shaped by the three components of the thought process: Wisdom and common sense, or *Hokhmah*; understanding, or *Binah*; and knowledge, or *Daat*.

True wisdom, to the mystic, is the common sense of practicality. A story about King Solomon illustrates this idea. Once, he brought the wisest, most admired and successful men of his kingdom together in a single room. "Upon this door," said the king, "are ten of the best locks in the world. They have been designed by the cleverest locksmiths of the land. The first one of you who can open the locks and walk through the door will become my chief minister."

When the king left the room and closed the door behind him, some of the more mechanically-minded began sketching each of the ten locks. Some decided to put their heads together to fashion a means of cooperative escape. Others began looking for tools or keys that might be hidden in the room. One just sat back, pondered the king's words, studied what everyone else in the room was doing and finally just went to the door, pushed it open and walked through.

Many smart people are not wise enough to just push open the door of life. They don't understand that their thinking needs to be grounded in common sense. Sometimes, just doing what needs to be done is the key to wisdom. Being able to think means to first be practical.

A Yiddish proverb makes the same point: "No one should test the depth of the river with both feet." "Look before you leap" is a modern version of that. Wise carpenters address this issue by telling their apprentices "measure twice, and cut once."

Thinking should have two components: The experiences that shaped our lives, and simple common sense. The mystics tell us that we have to combine this personal, practical wisdom with understanding, which comes from study over time and from serious reasoning. The result is knowledge, which guides our journey to happiness.

Here's a final story that may knit together all of these ideas. A king once owned the most precious diamond in the world. It was huge and flawless, with hundreds of facets that reflected light in a rainbow of colors.

Each evening, the king took the diamond from his safe, unwrapped it and examined it by the light of the moon or stars, marveling at its beauty. One morning, after he dreamed that the diamond had sustained a large scratch, he nervously removed the gem from its wrappings. The diamond dropped to the floor. When he picked it up, the king saw a large scratch marring the surface of the gem.

Calling every jeweler in his kingdom, he offered a great reward to anyone who could restore the diamond to its pristine perfection. Hundreds of craftsmen examined it and determined that not only couldn't the stone be restored, but that it was worthless in its current condition. A magician promised to turn back time, but failed. A chemist bathed the stone in various solutions to no avail.

Finally, an artist from another land who was visiting a friend heard of the king's plight. He examined the diamond and pledged to repair the gem to an even greater beauty than before it was scratched. The king was skeptical, but let the artist take the diamond for several weeks.

When the young man returned, the king looked at his gem and was astounded. On the top of the scratch, the artist had carved a magnificent rosebud. At the center of the scratch, he had fashioned a delicate leaf. This rose carved in diamond reflected and refracted light in even more beautiful ways than the unmarred stone. Its value skyrocketed, and it became the talk of the kingdom.

Think of the fable as a metaphor for our own process of thinking.

The diamond is our soul.

The scratch is an event or inclination that seemingly can ruin our lives.

The jewelers are those who would discourage us and make us feel that our plight is hopeless.

The magicians and chemists are the hucksters who offer quick solutions to life's long-term problems.

The artist is our ability to visualize what can be and then

to use our common sense and the skills we have learned through study to make the good thing happen.

This is the path we must follow to find happiness within.

Exercises for the Soul

Monday   Think of two negative passions or attitudes that have hurt you in the past. Write them down on a sheet of paper that you keep in your pocket until Tuesday.

Tuesday   Take out the piece of paper. Under each of the negative passions or attitudes you've listed, write down a single time and place that it has hurt you or led you astray. Fold up the paper and take it with you wherever you go.

Wednesday   Take out the piece of paper and pretend that it holds each of the negative passions listed on it. As you have carried around this piece of paper, so, too, have you carried around these passions. Make a conscious effort to control your passions. Remove yourself from your automatic pilot. Put your negative passion on hold.

Thursday   Make a list of two things that you want to do on Friday and Saturday that will take no more than two hours, but will help you feel better about yourself or your life. Close your eyes and see yourself preparing to do each of these things, then actually doing them and finally finishing each.

Friday
Now, do the first of the two things that you listed on Thursday. Attempt to do it just as you envisioned it. Go through each step. Don't berate yourself if you stumble. Just keep going. Celebrate when you finish.

Saturday
Do the second thing you listed on Thursday. Try to do it just as you envisioned. Go through each step. Remember, try to get it right. If you get 75 percent of the way there, you're doing just fine. Celebrate in whatever way you'd like once you finish. Read a book; see a film; have dinner at your favorite restaurant.

Sunday
Look at the paper with your negative passions. If you have experienced them less than usual this week, celebrate and tear the paper in half. Next week, carry only one half of the sheet and repeat this process until the paper is too small to tear.

CHAPTER 4

WANTING IT MORE; ENJOYING IT LESS

We must make a decision, and the choice is ours: Poverty, pain, illness and despair; or wealth, pleasure, health and optimism?

This is a trick question. Although few of us knowingly choose misery over comfort, many people make just this sort of bad decision in spiritual and intellectual matters. Mystics, in fact, believe that we tend to drift toward negativity, that a brooding darkness is basic to human nature. Like electrical sparks attracted to a metal object, the negative sparks of our thoughts are attracted to the very foundation of our thought process.

The pods or shells that contain these negative sparks, which are called *Kelipot,* cause low self-esteem and insecurity and can become the major obstacle to a joyful life. As with any source of energy, they can wreak havoc if not controlled. Unharnessed, their unpredictable power can loom at the corner of our consciousness until they surge, like lightning striking a neighborhood power line, and cripple vital circuits.

Yet, *Kelipot* can be harnessed, regulated and turned into a phenomenal source of self-esteem, achievement and joy. The ability to do that is an essential part of a healthy spirituality.

To understand how to control our *Kelipot*, it is vital to understand the nature and source of this important life energy. Negative sparks are not born with us; they are made for us, often by the people we love most. A miserable person with a sense of humor might wryly comment that misery comes naturally to many of us, because we were trained by experts at a young age. Our mothers and fathers, teachers and friends built the "circuits" for our negative sparks, wiring and maintaining each connection, day after day, year after year, until we became convinced that every success was, in fact, a failure, or at best short-lived, and that winning wasn't really that satisfying anyway.

Insecurity Burns Away Our Spiritual Centers

If we look back, we may find someone, seemingly innocent and well-meaning, who built the infrastructure for your misery. These unintending angels of death, or *Malakh Hamaves*, resemble a woman I know named Mrs. Kay. Her friends point to her with pride. A fine mother, they say. So involved with her children and grandchildren. So caring. But look closer.

It is true that Mrs. Kay has never physically abused her children. Nor would she ever imagine doing so. The damage she's done, however, is as devastating as any scars left behind by a parent wielding a belt.

Mrs. Kay's children are very bright. When they brought home report cards with straight A's, she would wrinkle her nose, shake her head slowly from side to side, sigh and wonder why there was not a single A+

Certainly, her motives were honorable. What parent does not want their child to do better? But Mrs. Kay made it clear that no matter how well her children did, it was never good enough.

When they started careers and proudly told their mother about a salary increase they were expecting, Mrs. Kay would make those familiar signs of displeasure and tell her children about cousin Sheppy, who had just received a deferred compensation package that would make him rich one day. Her children would buy a wonderful new home, and Mrs. Kay would point out that the schools were better in another neighborhood. Her grandchildren would paint her a special picture for her birthday, and she would talk about her cousin Helen's grandchildren, who were so bright, so advanced for their ages.

Mrs. Kay was surprised when I asked why her children's accomplishments never seemed good enough for her. "I'm very proud of my children," she said, "but they need to strive to do better. They must never be satisfied with what they have."

Her attitude was designed to motivate her children to "make sure they are never lazy." While perhaps it could be argued that she succeeded, anyone who knows her children can easily see their unhappiness, their insecurity, their low self-regard. Without meaning to do so, Mrs. Kay manufactured the negative sparks that burned away the spiritual center of her children's lives.

Bring Happiness by Setting Reasonable Goals

Negative sparks come in three varieties. Each has distinct characteristics, but all can be addressed with a common plan to harness them for positive purposes.

The first variety, insatiability, is sometimes prized by the most successful and intense people in the world. Whether the desire is power, money, sex or food, human nature often pushes us to want more. Can we ever have too much love? Or even enough? Can a child ever get too much attention, receive too many hugs or too many words of encouragement? Do you know anyone who would ever say, "I'm good looking enough. No clothing, no haircut, no makeup or exercise program can make me any more wonderful than I am already?" Have you ever met someone who says, "I have all the money I want"...and actually means it?

This negative energy is so prevalent that the mystics believed it created more unhappiness and dissatisfaction than any other. It is easy to understand why, because if the sky is indeed the limit, there can be no boundaries, there can be no goals, there can be no sense of completion.

And without these, there can be no joy.

Being insatiable is the stuff of tragedy. From the legend of King Midas who never had enough gold to satisfy his greed, to the myth of Sisyphus, who was cursed to push a boulder up a mountain only to watch it roll back down, human storytellers understood that suffering accompanies the inability to achieve a reachable goal.

A modern version of the Sisyphus myth might be the entrepreneur who works his entire life to accumulate wealth and finally makes the bottom of *Forbes* magazine's list of the world's richest people. This man doesn't see his achievement, because he can't turn his gaze away from those above him on the *Forbes* list. Are they looking down scornfully at him, he wonders? Are they laughing because he is last?

What can this entrepreneur do, what can any of us do, to turn this negativity into positive energy that brings happiness and joy? Mystical Jewish texts offer a three-pronged transformational approach:

- Be realistic.
- Be persistent.
- Seek a conclusion.

A balanced approach to life, what mystics called *Tiferet,* makes such practical sense that it's surprising so few of us practice it. If we can't be the richest person in the world, why even try to be? Because the effort will make us miserable? The logic against it is simple, but compelling.

As a practical strategy, why not aim for a goal that's near the top, not at the top. If inner contentment is important, set professional goals at 75 percent of what's possible. About 7.5 out of 10 can be done most of the time. This reasonable number doesn't discourage effort by being too low, nor invite failure by being too high. The approach works equally well with affairs of the heart, with beauty, with anything that you feel compelled to push toward an endlessly elusive target.

Wall Street traders have a wonderful expression that is inspired by the "7.5 rule." They say: "Bulls get rich. Bears get rich. Pigs get slaughtered." In the jargon of the Street, the first rule for transforming your negative sparks is: Don't be a pig.

The second step in the transformation of *Kelipot* is persistence, or what the Kabbalist would call splendor or *Hod*. Once we set an achievable goal, we must pursue it. If it's really important, we can't stop, be waylaid or lose focus. Because the goal is now realistic, a reasonable timetable that we adhere to will set us up for success.

Finally, we must bring our effort to a conclusion, or *Netzah*. Sales people call it "closing a deal." Psychologists call it finding closure. I describe it as a celebration. Once we reach a goal, we can't be afraid to enjoy it, to give ourselves a gift, throw a party, brag a little. We can't let our angels of death minimize what we've accomplished. Rather than feeling we are only as good as our next miracle, we can relax a little and feel the power of this moment of accomplishment.

Even Our Heroes Struggle for Happiness

We must understand that each time we achieve a goal, we are a step closer to inner fulfillment. Every time we deliver on a commitment to ourselves, we are nearer to being at one with the universe. Setting realistic goals, persisting until we achieve them and enjoying our accomplishments is an essential part of reaching completeness and true joy.

Just as we set ourselves up for failure with the negative spark of insatiability, so too do we create impossible odds when we start comparing ourselves to others. Perhaps we began doing this as children, when we compared ourselves to our mothers and fathers, only to discover that the strength and wisdom of adulthood is something that a child can't have. Or maybe it was our efforts to be like the heroes of comic books and literature, whose bravery, honesty and sophistication we could never match. It was in those ways that a sense of inferiority was etched into even our childhood fantasies.

As adults, we don't do much better. We believe the messages implied in magazine stories about celebrities, powerful leaders, and the best and brightest, printed beside those about failures and broken people. And we wonder which category we fall into.

The lives of the rich and famous seem more grand than our own. The plight of those who have failed then becomes a chilling reminder of how much closer we are to the bottom than to the top. But we have no idea what the lives of our heroes and heroines are really like. The stories we read are frequently engineered by well-paid publicists whose goal is to sell albums or books or movie tickets. Their clients wake up with bad hair, bad breath and bad attitudes, but don't expect a camera to record any of it. When stars fall in public view, we finally understand that they are as flawed as any of us. Yet, we dutifully move our affection and attention to another seemingly unflawed creation of the publicist's machine.

The same process applies to people closer to home. There's always a relative whom we assume is better or a neighbor whom we assume has a better love life or a co-worker who has an inside track on a promotion because of his or her color, faith or golf handicap. All of this seems clear to us, because, as with most delusions, we exclude information from our thinking that may cast doubt on our beliefs.

But an old proverb advises, "The happiest people I know are the ones I don't know very well." With that in mind, here's a story about a man who suffered from terrible depression. He went to see a great psychiatrist and told him that he saw only misery in the faces of the people he saw on the street, and that everything he did made him more despondent.

Listening thoughtfully, the psychiatrist confided to the patient that he, too, at times became depressed from interacting with so many troubled people. "But," he said, "whenever I feel blue I go to see the comedian, Rosario, the funniest man in the world. I envy him, because he has the world at his feet. So many love and respect him. I try to think the way Rosario would think, and suddenly I become cheerful. So, go to see Rosario. I guarantee that will be all the treatment you need."

"But doctor," the patient replied. "*I* am Rosario."

Let's use the mystics' three-step approach to convert this negative tendency to compare ourselves to others into something that works to enhance our lives.

First, find someone you respect who lives a life you find meaningful and rewarding. Choose someone accessible and real to you, rather than someone profiled in magazines. Now, try to determine what makes the person's life seem so special. This process of demystification, *Tiferet,* makes things realistic. Do traits that make this person seem special stem from their success, their money or their notoriety? Or from their intelligence, creativity or kindness?

The failure to look closely at our role models and the tendency to imitate only obvious traits can be disastrous. Consider the tragic story of Freddy Prince, who had become one of the nation's best-known comics before he killed himself in his twenties. He used the bittersweet humor of his poverty-stricken youth in the Bronx to create a unique voice in American humor. His nightclub act was a smash, and he landed a role on a television sitcom. Thousands of young people around the nation read about him in magazines and newspapers and believed that if only they could get a break the way Freddy Prince did, they, too, could be hugely successful.

The problem was that Freddy Prince never realized he had made it. On each step of his long climb to success, he'd brought along that poor kid from the Bronx. His inner child was still not convinced that Freddy was as good as everyone said he was. In fact, Prince had patterned his performance skills after the funniest men of his childhood. He had memorized their routines, their timing, their facial expressions, every aspect of their public faces. But he had never had a chance to look at them closely enough to understand their lives and how they had found inner joy from their work and success.

Perhaps if he had, he would have been able to believe that he was really as good as everyone said he was. He might have been able to enjoy some of his success. He might not have killed himself.

Getting to know a role model can be difficult, but we should try. Create a pattern of persistence, of splendor or *Hod,* that allows you to learn from your role model. Ask the person to be your mentor. Explain your respect and admiration, and there's a good chance you'll have a friend for life.

If our role model is a figure from history, or is not personally accessible, we can study that individual through books and other resources. We should approach this process the way we might handle a research project for school or work.

Joy Comes from Following Our Dreams— and Helping Others Follow Theirs

We bring things to closure, or *Netzah,* by taking ownership of the positive, desirable traits we've uncovered.

President Bill Clinton has frequently discussed his youthful ambition and his pursuit of success. As a youth, he studied the lives of his heroes and discovered that they all had a few traits in common. One of the easiest to imitate was their ability to function with less sleep than the average person. They tended to go to sleep late each night and awake early the next morning. So, Clinton trained himself to get by with just five hours of sleep, using the extra time as his role models did: To study, read or plan.

Our tendency to compare ourselves to others is closely related to the third mystical negative spark: Seeing through the limited eyes of others. A wonderful story illustrates how this negative spark can blind us to life's possibilities.

Lauren, a second grader, had an unusual answer to a question posed by her teacher. "Describe what apples look like," the teacher asked after a visit to a nearby orchard. One child raised her hand and said she'd seen many red apples. Another reported that there were quite a few green apples, too. A third added yellow to the list of colors. "Anything else," the teacher asked. Lauren's hand went up.

"White," Lauren said. "I saw white apples."

Her classmates giggled. Her teacher frowned, saying, "Certainly you don't mean white?" Lauren said that every apple she'd seen had been white. Her classmates' laughter grew, and the teacher's frustration grew with it. She warned Lauren to stop fooling around.

But Lauren persisted, the laughter grew, and the teacher sent her to the principal, who also asked: "What color were the apples?" Again, Lauren answered, "White." The principal grew annoyed and called Lauren's parents to school, suggesting that their child either was being insubordinate or had something very wrong with her vision.

Lauren's father kneeled beside her and said, "I don't think I've ever seen an apple that wasn't red, green or yellow. Where did you see a white one?" Through her tears, the child answered, "They were all white, Daddy. They were all white—inside."

Lauren was able to resist the pressure to see the world through the limited eyes of others. Many of us are not. We let others define or judge our lives. Greatness, whether in the arts or sciences, politics or business, is achieved through individuality. Being able to see things before others do or see what others simply cannot, is one of the fundamental characteristics of greatness and happiness. Great people and happy people not only see things their own way, they also won't let others argue or bully them into conforming to more widely held views.

Mystics believe that we should not let others toss cold water on a hot idea or belittle an unfamiliar one. They would counsel that we must follow our dreams, because it is our dreams that have the potential to make the world a better, more kind and beautiful place. These dreams, gifts from God, are worth pursuing.

In fact, acquiring inner joy can be advanced by finding other people who understand and share our dreams, and then helping them identify their own. We create positive energy by helping others understand that, while their needs may be insatiable, they can find satisfaction in achieving a goal set at 7.5 out of 10, and that having a unique vision should be cherished, not trashed.

When we share our success and when we empower others to celebrate themselves, we help them make their lives fuller. That can fill our lives with joy. A helping hand can become a bridge for two souls to be partners in true spiritual living, in what the mystics call *tikkun olam,* or the communal act of repairing the world. This can assume all kinds of dimensions, both expected and unexpected.

Exercises for the Soul

Monday   List three things you'd like to achieve this year. Be specific. For example, if one goal is financial, state the amount you'd like to earn.

Tuesday   Think through the specifics of each goal you listed Monday and make a reasonable effort to lower your expectations by 25 percent. These are your final goals.

Wednesday   List specific things you can do to reach each goal. Will taking a certain class get you the raise you want or the promotion you crave? Will exercising each morning for one hour help you lose ten pounds? Create a specific plan for each goal. In the months ahead, stick to it.

Thursday   Think about why certain people are your role models. List two traits that make each person special to you. List two traits that you do not admire. If you can't do these things, do some research to learn more about these people.

Friday   Identify as many things about yourself as you can that you've altered to meet the expectations of others. Be honest.

Saturday   Identify your unique vision. What do you see or understand about the world that is special and different from the crowd? Reflect about why you received this gift.

Sunday   Spend 30 minutes just listening to another person. Try to hear the pain in their lives. Perhaps then you can help them understand it.

CHAPTER 5

GETTING THROUGH THE PAIN

If life could be a fairy tale, it might resemble the one lived by a woman named Pam. Her life was magical and blessed, a constant stroll on a sunny afternoon through a warm wooded glen.

But, like many a fairy tale, a beast was lurking behind the trees, and the forest beyond the glen was dark and dangerous.

Pam's father was wealthy, and her mother doted on her. Her husband, Henry, was successful and attentive, and they had a son and daughter. Pam had an advanced degree in music and frequently played her violin at local concerts.

As her father was reaching retirement age, he convinced Pam's husband to become a partner in his successful law practice. In a few years, a rift developed between the two men. Henry opened his own office, taking the firm's largest accounts with him and leaving his father-in-law's business in ruin.

Pam did not take sides, despite the efforts of her father and husband. Her father made a convincing case that Henry was dishonest and underhanded; Henry was equally convincing when he argued that the older man was controlling and old-fashioned. Had he not left the firm, Henry said, his own career would have crashed with the father-in-law's firm. Then where would he and Pam have been?

When Pam's father had a stroke several months later, Pam's fairy tale existence began to change even more. She spent much time caring for her father, while Henry began spending more time at the office. When Henry did come home, he would talk more about the paralegal at his office who "was like a daughter to him" than he would talk to his own children. Pam's father died a short time after his stroke. Three weeks later, Henry filed for divorce.

This much loss arriving at one time into a life that had known nothing but success and joy was more than Pam could handle. She was inconsolable, confused, angry. When Henry announced plans to marry his paralegal, Pam became bitter. Friends would hear endless harangues about Henry or tearful memories of her father. When couples took her to dinner or to parties, they would sit through an evening of Henry-bashing. Soon, people stopped calling, and the dinner invitations dwindled.

Friends searched for ways to help Pam. The chairman of the music department at a local university offered her a teaching position; she was invited to join a professional quartet. She passed on all these, saying she was too busy with her divorce. At first, the children supported their mother, refusing even to speak with Henry. They called him "the killer" and his new wife "the whore."

But as Pam grew more bitter, she even accused her children of seeing their father on the sly or not sufficiently supporting her needs. Her son's grades plummeted. Within a year, he dropped out of college. Her daughter began spending more time sleeping at a girlfriend's house than at home. Within two years of her divorce settlement, both children were living with their father—and Pam was alone.

Now, a decade after the divorce, Pam is still obsessed with her ex-husband. She says her friends deserted her because "Henry had gotten to them." At cocktail parties, Henry tells the latest "Pam story," describing how she spends nights in her car watching his driveway. Her children think their mother has gone off the deep end and have begun calling Henry's wife "mom." Pam insists they have been bought off, just like her former friends.

"I'm a good person," Pam says. "Why is this happening to *me*? He ruined *my* life. He killed *my* father and stole his business. He took everything from *me*. I can't let him get away with what he's done—to *me*."

Cultivating the Strength to See Good

Emotional pain is as debilitating as physical pain. It drags us into a place without apparent escape. It is easy to be consumed by it and to wallow in the loneliness and rage that it creates. When we're in pain, we tend to see everything through its filter. Faced with catastrophe, sickness and death, even the strongest among us can become weak. Misshapen by a moment's tragedy, we can fall victim to a disaster that lasts a lifetime.

It doesn't have to be that way. A Yiddish proverb states, "To a worm in horseradish, the whole world is horseradish." In other words, to those in pain the whole world is filled with painful things. But if we find options to a life mired in the anger and self-pity, we can find that elusive inner joy.

Once, a man visited an internationally renowned rabbi seeking truth, fulfillment and joy. After hours of convincing the scholar of his sincerity and willingness to learn, the rabbi showed the young man a cellar lined with books.

"This is where you will eat and sleep," the rabbi said. "If you wish to find the answers to your questions, you must read each one of these books. I shall visit you each day, and you will tell me what you have gleaned from their pages. I will then teach you what you need to know."

Each day at dinner time, the rabbi went to the basement room. Each day, the young man recounted what he'd read. The rabbi would then give a brilliant commentary. Once a week, the young man would relate what the rabbi had taught him to what he had gleaned from each book, and how that related to the other volumes he had read.

The rabbi would say, "Good!" Then he would strike the young man on the head with a cane. The ritual was repeated each week for years.

Finally, the young man read every book in the cellar. After he gave his recitation of the final book and how it related to all that the rabbi had taught him, the rabbi said, "Good" and lifted the cane. But before the cane could strike him, the young man grabbed the rabbi's hand. "Rebbe, I have finished the books, and I have done all you've asked.

Do not hit me again."

"Ah," said the rabbi, "this is very good. You see, my son, you have not just learned the lessons of the books. You have learned that it is in your power to stop the pain! Now, you may begin to live your life."

To mystics, with all wisdom comes the realization that we have the power to control our reactions to the things life brings us. It is childish to believe that we can control what happens. We can't make the rabbi stop raising his cane to strike us, but we can grab his hand before he brings it down across our back. We do not control what happens to us, but we can control how we react. This is essential to stopping the pain in our lives.

Once we acquire this understanding, we can begin the process described by mystics to conquer that pain. The first step is achieving a sense of what mystics call strength, or *Gevurah*, which is the ability to take control of ourselves mentally and focus on the positive possibilities of our lives. When you feel frustration, anger, self-pity or fear, *Gevurah* helps you realize that those negative emotions are counterproductive and will not help make things right. They do not bring back a loved one or stop the spread of a disease. Instead, anxiety and panic can be overcome by forcing ourselves to be positive and hopeful.

Ancient mystics knew that controlling ourselves in moments of anger or agony is among the hardest things we can do, hence the name *Gevurah*. It requires strength. Once we can stifle the tendency to strike out at others or to retreat into self-pity during the worst times of our lives, we become the master of our grief. With the energy created by focusing on the positive pieces of our world, we can confront and gain control of our pain, rather than let it control us.

Transforming Sorrow to Joy

The second and complementary step to *Gevurah* is called grace, or *Chesed*: The ability and willingness to be kind and to do good things even when faced with the worst situations in life.

What is *Chesed*? Instead of wallowing in her sorrow, a woman who lost her child to a drunk-driving accident started an organization called Mothers Against Drunk Driving. MADD is now a major influence in shaping legislation and public awareness of the dangers of drinking and driving. That is *Chesed*. A woman in Detroit whose young son was killed in the crossfire of a gang shooting could have lashed out at the unfairness of urban life and fled with her family to safer environs. Instead, she started Save Our Sons and Daughters, a group dedicated to eradicating violence among the young. That is *Chesed*, a good, graceful thing coming from one's deepest grief.

Can *Chesed* be achieved in a more personal and private way? A man who had a reputation in business as being hardheaded and tough developed a life-threatening illness. Instead of cursing the doctors or being angry at those who were healthy, he trimmed his working hours and began volunteering for various charitable organizations. His new charm and humor delighted people. Something else happened. His family called it a miracle; his doctors couldn't explain it any better. He recovered his health. This is *Chesed*.

To the person whose losses are immeasurable, kindness may seem an inappropriate response. But because it creates a sudden, yet subtle feeling of well-being, mystics understand that it is precisely the best response to sorrow.

Mystics believed that when *Chesed* and *Gevurah* are both within the shattered heart, something more satisfying than joy develops. This harmony, or *Tiferet,* is felt when we are at one with ourselves and our world. Once we experience it, there's no escaping its lure. Once we know the pleasure of *Tiferet,* we understand that even through loss and disease we can make our lives satisfying and more loving. That supernatural sensation of harmony is so powerful, so mystical, that we want to experience it, again and again.

But four obstacles can prevent the mystical formula of *Gevurah* (strength and positive focus) plus *Chesed* (kindness) to arrive at *Tiferet.* Feeling harmony and pleasure in the face of pain isn't easy because we make such excuses as:

How can we feel good about ourselves without being disloyal to those we have lost? While this urge is very powerful, it is important to understand that people who love us do not wish us to be unhappy. Instead, they would hope we can carry on their memories in a positive, productive way.

How can we move beyond illness when we've been trained by parents and society that for people to believe we are sick, we must act sick? This falsehood can make us even sicker. If we want to stifle our bodies' immune response to disease, there's no better way than to act sick and bemoan our every ache and pain. Mystics don't teach us that, modern medicine does. Playing above the pain is a characteristic of great athletes; not focusing on an illness is a characteristic of a healthy soul.

Isn't it human to expect everyone around us to feel badly out of respect for our pain? The cliché "misery loves company" certainly is true. But a reasonable person who thinks this expectation through quickly understands that the last thing a sick person wants is to share their sickness with others they love. Would any of us wish cancer or mourning or a debilitating condition on those we hold dear? Why create negative energy that will only make us sicker or more sad?

We expect perfection, and when disease, death and pain occur, the world seems grossly unfair. These things should not happen in a perfect world. If they do, it suggests that the world is far from perfect or that we are somehow flawed and apart from our perfect world.

Perfectionist thinking is the most difficult hurdle to overcome in our efforts to achieve harmony in the face of disease or tragedy. In a perfect world, good people should never have a problem. Storybook lives should continue until the end of time. The frogs we kiss should all become princes or princesses. Intellectually, we know that this view of the world is flawed. Most of the time when we kiss a frog, it stays a frog. We understand this intellectually, but in our hearts we believe otherwise.

Expecting perfection poisons our minds and our souls. How can we feel *Gevurah* (strength) when we are suddenly presented with the possibility of a less than perfect world? We must understand, emotionally and intellectually, that there are no perfect people or perfect situations. There are only perfect fantasies.

Once, a rabbi prayed daily that God would make a perfect world in which there would be no hatred, jealousy, pain or problems. One night, God appeared to the rabbi in a dream and took him on a tour of the world made perfect.

The rabbi saw his house, his synagogue, his town. Lions and lambs laid down together. Still, the rabbi was troubled. Something was missing. "Where am *I* in this perfect world?" the rabbi asked. God offered an apologetic answer: "This is the perfect world you requested. You must understand that you are not perfect, so you cannot be included."

The Talmud is very clear about this. Because the world is not perfect, it is neither fair nor unfair. It is just time and space that we must fill with the best we have. We must strive to live our lives well. The alternative is to let the world go by while we just curse fate, God and whatever else comes to mind. Neither anger nor tears make the world a better place.

We all must realize that things happen in life to make us feel bad, but that they have no relationship to how we live our lives. A very wise man once said that expecting the world to treat us fairly because we are nice people is like expecting the bull not to gore us just because we're vegetarians.

We enter dangerous ground when we convince ourselves that we are victims. This feeling begins a chain of negative thinking that culminates in believing that feeling bad is the right thing to feel. We assume that our lives should mirror the perfect images in our imaginations, that we should be just like the rich and famous we see in our media. We make everything worse for ourselves by believing that we are not as good as we should be. It is not unusual for very rational people to say that they should be above disease or death, that their fine lives qualify them for preferential treatment. This belief is implied whenever people wonder, "Why did God do this to me?" or "Why is this happening to me? What did I do wrong?" These are the laments of the victim trapped in perfectionist thinking, the refrain of people who feel wronged by fate or those certain that there are others whose lives, indeed, are perfect.

To a man without substantial assets, perhaps money can make him immune to life's caprice. Or, more likely, as F. Scott Fitzgerald said, "Money doesn't make you better. It just helps you live better."

An unmarried person might assume that marital bliss will guard them against misery. Certainly, people don't feel this way because they know so many happily married couples. In truth, the happiest married people are those who were happy before marriage.

The Jewish mystics had a simple belief: Not only does perfection not exist, but pain and pleasure are both part of life. When we experience pain, the whole world seems painful. When we are happy, the world is a bed of roses; when sad, a handful of thorns. To the mystic, it is a combination of both. What is real is what we focus on. The thorns will always be on the rose's stem. Indeed, slicing the thorns off the stem shortens the life of the flower.

Jewish mystics believe, though, that we must focus our attention on the flower. Our job is not to make the world perfect or to expect perfection, because the Messiah will do this. While we wait for the Messiah, we are obligated to fix what is wrong in this life. By lessening our own pain, the world becomes a better place.

When God Closes a Door, God Opens a Window

Consider the life of an ordinary woman who made the world better, not by writing a book or creating a worthwhile social organization, but by resuming a useful and fulfilling life in the face of substantial obstacles. Sharon had a lot for which to be thankful. Her parents were alive and well. She and her family had recently moved to an upscale suburban house near her childhood home after her husband had been transferred from New York to a top corporate job in the Midwest. She and her family enjoyed health, prosperity and a sense of well-being that Sharon described as happiness.

Then her good life seemed to disintegrate. Her father called from Florida to tell Sharon that her mother had ovarian cancer. Sharon's husband encouraged her to travel to Florida to be with the woman she had always called her best friend. It was reassuring to Sharon that her husband was so willing to take care of himself and their daughters in this time of trouble. He'd never been this supportive in their 13 years of marriage.

Within a month, her mother was dead. Several weeks later, Sharon's husband quit his new job, explaining that his recent relocation had not been a promotion, but an attempt to move him away from the New York office, where he had been having an affair with a co-worker. No longer able to live without his lover, he'd found a job in New York and was leaving immediately. He even asked her to tell their children the news.

A few weeks after her husband left, Sharon was still sobbing. "I didn't just lose my mother and my husband," she said. "I lost my trust, too. Things aren't supposed to happen this way."

For months, Sharon fell into such terrible depressions that some of her new neighbors called me for help. A few days after we'd spoken briefly by phone, she appeared in my office unannounced. She seemed no longer depressed, not even angry.

Instead, she was afraid. The divorce papers she had just received told her that it would be months before any support would come from her estranged husband. This forced her to begin looking at what possibilities life could now offer. She and I spent some time on the phone, looking for opportunities.

Three days later, a friend who was selling a retail business asked if Sharon wanted to buy it. Although Sharon wasn't interested in running a store, she did see this as an opportunity to get control of her life. She soon found a buyer for her friend's business. The sales commission that Sharon received from her friend provided the capital for Sharon to start a company that matched sellers of businesses with buyers.

She used high school friends, neighbors and old roommates to help get a business bought and sold for the highest dollar. Whenever she finished a transaction, she sent letters and baskets of fruit to everyone who helped her. When I asked who had taught her to do business that way, she answered: "My mom did *life* that way. All I did was apply her philosophy to doing business. After all, it was really my mom who got me through this whole thing. After I sat around moaning all day about how unfair everything was, I remembered that my Mom used to tell me that God doesn't do fair. God gives you opportunities. When God closes a door, God opens a window.

"When I wasn't just thinking about me and my problems and found a way to help someone else, I knew Mom was making God open a room full of windows. All I had to do was fly through one of them."

Sharon had learned the lessons of the mystics well. By combining the strength and focus of *Gevurah* with the kindness and grace of *Chesed*, she achieved *Tiferet*. Her spiritual harmony helped her stop the pain, take charge of her life and begin living again.

For those of us who believe in fairy tales, this is the true definition of living happily ever after.

Exercises for the Soul

Monday	Write down these words: "I will not be a victim." Do not let anyone make you feel that you do not control how you act and react. Keep the paper with those words where you can see it during the day.

Tuesday	Silently repeat the words, "Be strong." Whenever you feel emotional pain, do not let it control you. You are no longer a victim.
Wednesday	Repeat the words, "I am strong enough to be kind." Write a letter or make a call to someone you care about, and tell that person how much he or she means to you.
Thursday	Repeat again, "I am strong enough to be kind." Write a letter or make a call to someone you think you may have hurt. Tell that person you are sorry, and try to win a friend.
Friday	Turn every "no" into a "yes." Instead of criticizing what is wrong, find something that is right in everybody and in everything that you encounter.
Saturday	Write down what makes you angry. For the rest of the day, each time you face a triggering event, don't let your anger overwhelm you.
Sunday	Be kind to others for the entire day. In the evening, go to a private place and figuratively pat yourself on the back.

CHAPTER 6

MAKING SUCCESS AND AMBITION WORK FOR YOU

A lawyer I know named Harry mounted that famous quote on his office wall, the one by the legendary coach of the Green Bay Packers, Vince Lombardi—"Winning isn't everything. Winning is the *only* thing." Harry had two goals in life: To head a law firm and to join the most prestigious country club in town. He worked hard and achieved those goals.

Yet, he was depressed: "I'm the head of the firm, and now everybody and their brother comes to me with their problems and their complaints. I belong to this nice club, and I can't stand three-quarters of the people there. I never see my friends because I'm too busy at the office. I like it, though, when I take someone to lunch and they are impressed that I belong to such a fancy club. But they should only know. I hate golf. The food is second-rate. And the people are cold fish.

"After 20 years of hard work," he wonders, "I'm not sure if this is what I wanted."

Harry is certainly not alone in asking that kind of question. Many powerful people, who are viewed by their peers and by society as great successes, question their success. Call it a mid-life crisis or a search for meaning, but contemporary adults commonly find themselves wondering whether they can consider themselves successful and whether success and happiness are in any way related.

Simply trying to define "success" is difficult. Does success mean we have attained a certain goal? Does it mean we are better than everyone else? Can it be measured by dollar signs and net worth? Perhaps those definitions are meaningless if the people we love and respect are not aware of what we've done—and if they do not appreciate it. We can wear ourselves out trying to reduce success to a catchy phrase or an easy-to-understand statement, and we may not come up with anything more meaningful than Vince Lombardi's bit of wisdom.

To Jewish mystics, efforts to define the fleeting, even tormenting concept of "success" is wasteful. They would instead prefer to discuss and consider how one can succeed. They might not reduce this process to a formula, but their thinking on this subject leads to just that—a formula for success.

A Formula for Success: Persistence, "A Fixed Time," Not Quitting, Attitude

The first ingredient in the formula is what the Kabbalist calls splendor, *Hod*. To attain splendor you must first be unwilling to give up in the face of significant obstacles. Simply put, you must have persistence. The mystics would say that just as an amateur sculptor hits a mallet against a chisel without apparent effect and grows frustrated when the stone does not chip, so success will elude the impatient. An expert sculptor will also hit his mallet against his chisel and produce no apparent effect. The expert, though, has a different expectation. The amateur's goal is to chip the stone; every blow that doesn't produce a chip is regarded as a failure. The expert's goal is to weaken the structure of the stone with each blow, so a chip will eventually break off. Each of the expert's blows is a success because he understands that form and beauty will emerge at the end of the long process.

There are countless examples in contemporary life of how successful people use *Hod* in their careers. Michael Jordan, perhaps the best basketball player ever to lace up a pair of sneakers, was cut from his high school football team. Sandra Day O'Connor, the first woman on the Supreme Court, was offered only one job, being a legal secretary when she graduated from law school. Norman Schwartzkopf, who led a triumphant force in the Gulf War, almost quit the military in bitterness over the Vietnam War.

If *Hod* can be reduced to a catchy phrase, we might say that those who fail in life pursue the path of least persistence.

The next necessary element of success is *Keva,* which roughly translates as "a fixed time." We must set aside time on a regular basis, the mystics say, to get the work done that is critical for success. Achievement is not created from random events nor is it built on sporadic inspiration. It is the result of doing each day what needs to be done. Trying to create a success by working when we can get around to it is doomed to fail. Working on a schedule day in and day out, month after month, is what leads to great rewards.

Woody Allen may have boiled down *Keva* to its pithy essence when he said that "90 percent of success is in just showing up."

If we patiently and deliberately work toward our goal, then, the mystics say, we are more likely to receive inspiration. This flash of ingenuity and brilliance is facilitated by consistently working toward a goal.

The third essential element to success is the ability to overcome all things, or *Netzah*. It is the unwillingness to let anything or anyone get us down. *Netzah* is the armor and wisdom we develop when we fail. It is an understanding that we will fail many times, and that our greatest glories occur when we try again after each failure. *Netzah* reminds us that true genius is the result of painful exertion, that practice and failure bring us closer to our goal.

After Thomas Edison had made 10,000 unsuccessful tests while trying to perfect the storage battery, a friend remarked, "Isn't it a shame that with all this tremendous labor you haven't been able to get any results." "Nonsense!" Edison answered. "I've got lots of results. I've discovered several thousand things that won't work."

Netzah might be a variation of another slogan popular with sports coaches: We are never beaten until we quit.

The final ingredient for success is attitude. Attitude is the "foundation," or *Yesod*. This lets us put the other pieces together and creates a will to win. It can make us unbeatable. When Israel's army faced Goliath with swords and shields, fleeing soldiers moaned, "He's so big. How can we win?" When David faced the same giant with nothing more than a crude slingshot, he said, "He's so big. How can I miss?"

Yesod gives you the ability to act as if you will surely succeed. It lets you believe in yourself and your ability, so that you *will* succeed. Attitude, we might say, determines altitude.

Six Warnings about Desiring Success

Now that we know the mystical approach, mystics themselves would caution us to use it with great care. These ingredients for success can unleash extremely powerful forces that may create a dangerous imbalance in our lives. Indeed, reaching success, which is known as the "kingdom" or *Malkhut,* was always considered the lowest level of the *Sefirot.* The ancients were convinced that the forces that could lead to success arose from the same impulses that are responsible for our sex drives and that the formula for success was similar to the one a lover should follow to keep a partner sexually attracted. To control a raging sex drive, rabbinic authorities would suggest replacing the sexual appetite with a taste for success. It is not clear how successful they were in replacing sex with that other "s-word," but mystics were as circumspect and cautious about success as they were about the dangers of sexual passion. So remember the following six cautions about desiring success.

Caution One: We must be careful what we wish for.

An extremely successful dentist is always angry because

he was never warned about "Caution One." He says, "I hate what I'm doing. I can't stand being in people's mouths all of the time. I hate waking up in the morning thinking my patients dislike seeing me because they are worried I might hurt them. The person I hate most of all is me as a 17-year-old boy, who decided I should become a dentist in the first place. When I went to college, what did I know? I thought dentists made a lot of money, and it was easy work. Now, here I am. Stuck."

Caution Two: If we don't truly enjoy what we're doing, "success" will be a living hell. There is no doubt that we will be miserable because we won't like the work required to be successful. This advice is even more poignant when a parent is trying to steer a child into a certain profession.

Consider the story of Dr. Frank, a well-known heart surgeon. He loved telling guests at his home that his father, a wonderful carpenter, had created much of the lovely furniture they saw around them. Dr. Frank would describe how his father retired and came to live in his house, and how he loved to baby-sit for the doctor's children and teach them how to carve and cut wood the old-fashioned way.

What he didn't say is that he was ashamed of his dad and only spoke of him after his death.

"He never had the time to teach me the trade," the surgeon recalled of his father. "He always regretted that, so he made amends by teaching my boys. My mother wanted me to become a doctor, and my father wanted me to be a carpenter. I compromised and became a surgeon. I still cut and saw and work with my hands, but I went to medical school to do it."

Several years after I first met Dr. Frank, he came to me in a funk. "My son wants to be a carpenter," Dr. Frank said angrily. "He's a pre-med junior at an Ivy League college, and wants to drop out and be a carpenter!"

He wanted me to talk with his son because he was horrified that the boy might become like his father, the man he was ashamed of. When the son came home from school on spring break, I had lunch with him: A very intense passionate young man who would not be deterred from his dream to be "an artist in wood."

"You don't understand, rabbi," he said. "School is like prison. I have the opportunity to study with a master craftsman. Whenever I work with wood, I come alive. I feel fantastic. I smell my Grandpa's pipe in my mind. It's like his hands are directing me."

Dr. Frank refused to support his son during his apprenticeship. Although they spoke regularly, he couldn't understand how his boy could have made such a dreadful mistake. To throw away a potential medical career to do what his grandfather had done was an embarrassment to Dr. Frank.

Several years later, the *New York Times* wrote about Dr. Frank's son, who was now considered the foremost furniture artist in the world. His pieces sell in the six figures. When I saw Dr. Frank a few days later, he had already made several hundred copies of the article to send to his friends.

"My father is laughing at me," he said. "When I started out in a career, all I wanted to be was comfortable and famous. I thought that if I were a surgeon I could achieve both. Who ever thought that you were supposed to enjoy work. Work was supposed to be work! You were supposed to hate it! My kid couldn't care less about success or fame or money. He just wants to enjoy what he's doing, and he is. He's got it all: Success, money, fame *and* he loves what he is doing."

Caution Three: We don't have to be world-class to be a success. As a Yiddish proverb says, "The woods would be very silent if no birds sang except the best."

Marvin is a perfect example of this idea. He has loved flying since his first trip to an airport as a child. He knows that he isn't the best pilot in the world—and not the worst, either. Not physically qualified to fly for the Air Force, he took flying lessons anyway and qualified to fly a number of sophisticated aircraft. He tracked down gadgets and accessories to make flying more enjoyable and more effective the way other people search for better golf clubs or the best fit in a running shoe.

Flying was Marvin's passion and his pastime. A power tool salesman by day and a connoisseur of things aeronautical by night, he acquired a reputation as someone a flyer could call for information about flying accessories and gear.

When the company he worked for was sold to a conglomerate that gave his territory to younger salesman, Marvin had no way to support his habit, much less his family. But he kept getting three or four calls a night from flying enthusiasts he had never met who had heard that he was a maven of the paraphernalia needed to look like, feel like and fly like a true pilot. His wife stated the obvious when he complained about not being able to find a new job: "You do a land office business in plane gadgets. Maybe you're not looking for a job because you've already found one."

Marvin began mailing newsletters to everyone in his pilot organization directories. Each newsletter contained unique products he'd located. Today, he publishes a semi-annual catalogue and realizes how lucky he is.

"I love getting up in the morning," he says. "I'm not just a working stiff anymore, at the beck and call of someone who pulls my strings. I still get a kick out of buying all of the newest and latest gizmos, I get a chance to do as much flying as I want. And I make a fortune."

Caution Four: No success or failure is final. Successes come and go. And come back again.

It is a lesson we learn with experience, but if we're made of the right material, a hard fall will result in a high bounce. Remember that thousands of people were sure Henry Ford would fail because he did not put a reverse gear in his first car.

Caution Five: Mystics don't fault people for their success, but they don't advocate the need to strive for it either. The reason is simple. Success is too ephemeral and transitory. People have short memories, after all, and it is human for others to wonder what we've done lately.

If we doubt the truth of this statement, consider this:

The most famous and successful person I ever met was the late Dr. Jonas Salk. I invited him to speak at a congregational meeting and was delighted when he accepted. While bragging to my congregants that I had arranged for the famous doctor to speak to us, a 25-year-old asked, "Who's Jonas Salk?" Incredulously, I answered, "He found the cure for polio!" The fellow innocently responded, "What's polio?"

Salk's contribution to health and society may be permanent. But the public's communal memory has been short, and the knowledge of subsequent generations has proven limited.

Challenge and Pleasure Are the Best Motivations

Caution Six: We don't need riches, fame or power to be successful.

The most successful people work hard because they want to. They are not motivated by money, power or fame, but by the sheer challenge and pleasure of their craft or profession.

Many people do extremely well in business, but never feel successful until they help with some project that gives them absolutely no material benefit. Some gifted, wealthy doctors, for instance, feel successful only after they participate in work in which they truly believe—work that may seem mundane and have only a marginal relationship to medicine. As George Washington Carver said, "When you can do the common things of life in an uncommon way, you will command the attention of the world."

Here's a wonderful story that illustrates this point. The richest man in a large eighteenth century town was inspecting his estate and reveling in all that he owned. Suddenly, he came across Yaakov.

"Why are you here, Yaakov, and why do you look so sad?" the richest man in town asked.

"My dear sir," Yaakov said. "God came to me in a terrible dream and whispered that the richest man in the town would die today. I wanted to tell you to take care of yourself, especially today."

The rich man laughed. "To tell you the truth, I have never felt better in my life. Nothing will happen to me, my friend."

Undeterred, Yaakov called, "Please, be careful," as the rich man rode away.

Soon, the richest man of the town began to think about Yaakov's dream. After all, he had always respected Yaakov for his kindness and the wonderful way he took care of those he loved. Yaakov was the most spiritual man in town, and he was rich in many mystical ways. So, as the morning wore on, he took what Yaakov said more and more seriously. The richest man in town finally went to his doctor, who told him he had the heart of a much younger man and should not worry about anything. He then went home for a quiet supper.

The next morning, he awoke, relieved that he was alive. He went for a stroll so everyone could see that he had not died, as Yaakov had prophesied.

He saw a huge crowd. Everyone was crying. "What's the matter," he called out. "What is happening here? I demand to know what has happened!" Someone in the crowd answered: "It's Yaakov. Yaakov died yesterday."

There's no easy way to communicate this notion of accomplishment other than to recall that rabbinic scholars urge us to remember the ten rules for getting rid of depression and becoming successful in the eyes of those who matter most in the world: First, go out and do something nice for someone else. Then, repeat the act nine times.

Then, remember that success, in itself, is a destination, but happiness is the process that takes us through the journey.

Exercises for the Soul

Monday
: Make a short list of all the things you could achieve if you put your mind to doing so. These should be things you would like to do, but for which you think you do not have the time.

Tuesday
: Choose one item from Monday's list. Take 30 minutes to envision yourself doing all the steps needed to complete this task. Now, write down these steps.

: (For example, if you want to learn Spanish, visualize yourself going to a book store and buying a book or a tape; setting aside a half hour every night to learn five words or phrases; repeating the words along with the tape; celebrating after finishing the first chapter of the book; feeling the sense of power and accomplishment in being able to speak Spanish; and moving on to the next chapter.)

Wednesday
: Start the project that you visualized on Tuesday.

Thursday
: Keep doing your project. Concentrate. Persist. Don't let anything discourage you.

Friday	Keep going. Look at how far you've already come. Don't look at how much you have left to do.
Saturday	Continue with the project. Tell someone you respect or you love about what you have done.
Sunday	Persist. Because you have accomplished a great deal, reward yourself with a celebration, such as dinner out or a new outfit.

CHAPTER 7

CREATING A ROAD MAP TO HAPPINESS

The path to happiness, mystics believe, is always right there in front of us. What they would call our life's path, or *B'shert,* ought to be quite simple to find. So simple, in fact, that most of us just look past it in search of something more complex, better hidden, less obvious.

Consider the story of Levi Yitzhak, the rabbi of Berdichev, Russia, who lived during the eighteenth century and found his life's treasure in an unexpected place.

The rabbi had a marvelous dream, one of those rare moments of absolute clarity that come during sleep. He dreamed that a fantastic treasure was buried near the gate of the Czar's palace at St. Petersburg. Because he was a Jew, he was prohibited from even going near the palace, but the dream was so vivid that he could not stay away.

He masqueraded as a Russian peasant and went to St. Petersburg to see if there was the slightest hope of retrieving the treasure. Once he arrived, his heart sank because the gate was guarded day and night. Levi maintained a clandestine vigil around the gate for several days, hoping that one of the guards might lose concentration or go to sleep and give him a brief moment in which to seize his treasure. Finally, the captain of the guards grew suspicious and confronted Levi Yitzhak. Hoping that the officer could help him find the treasure, the rabbi told him about the dream.

"You are wasting your time with dreams," the captain laughed. "I, too, had a dream about a treasure. I dreamed that an old woman who lived many years ago hid a treasure under her stove and died without telling anybody about it. In my dream, I visited a house in a town called Berdichev and went to a house owned by some Jewish fellow named Levi Yitzhak. Can you believe such a dream? Can you imagine a rich old lady living in a backwater town like Berdichev? How ridiculous that a treasure would be buried all these years and not be found by a man who lives right on top of it day and night? As for me, I don't pay any attention to these dreams. I advise that you do the same."

Levi Yitzhak rushed home and dug up the treasure. It was more than lucky for Levi that someone suggested he look for his fortune closer to home. It was his *B'shert*.

We Collaborate with God on Our Destiny

B'shert is a predestined path shaped by a combination of God's will and our own receptivity to opportunity, which will, during our lifetime, take us in directions not initially seen or anticipated.

Finding our path to happiness requires that we understand what the path is not: It is not predetermined. God does not completely control our destinies. Nor do we completely control them.

Are we then blank slates upon which we can draw our own path and shape our own lives? Or are we, as a computer engineer might say, "hard-wired" at birth with specific instructions that lead us to simply carry out the plan of another?

An ancient Hungarian proverb sheds light on this question and provides a metaphor for understanding the mystical concept of *B'shert*. "God gives every bird a worm. He just doesn't throw it into the nest."

Consider, now, a more contemporary story (and a true one) about a Catholic priest, Father Don, who worked as a chaplain at a large suburban hospital. His lifetime passion was professional baseball. As a child, he had memorized batting averages and collected trading cards; as an adult, his idea of a perfect day was going to the ballpark. In fact, he's been able to get a seat for every Detroit Tigers home game and spring training session. And somehow he's able to snag a seat to every World Series game, no matter where it is played.

Father Don developed his deliciously clever *B'shert* after listening to a big league scout complain that children from minority groups didn't play baseball because they lacked opportunities to get to the ballpark often enough. Without seeing the game up close, it was hard to fall in love with it. Father Don started a foundation that bought Detroit Tigers tickets for disadvantaged, inner-city kids. Father Don, of course, served as a willing chaperone.

By combining his job as a priest and his love for baseball, he raised significant contributions from patients at his hospital and endeared himself to the Tigers' front office. He even created a special fund to take a few terminal cancer patients to the World Series each year.

Father Don loves teasing himself about his "baseball gig." Beyond the jokes he understands how fortunate he is to be living his childhood fantasy, while helping hundreds of unfortunate kids.

To mystics, having fun while doing a good deed is exactly how God intended people to make themselves happy. The best kind of *B'shert* gives us a double dose of spiritual joy: Combining a personal passion with something that also brings peace or wholeness. It is a vehicle through which one can reach the highest of the *Sefirot:* The crown, or *Keter.*

Having fun while doing a good deed through our work rarely occurs. But those blessed with a joyful existence use their occupations as a way to pay the tolls on their path to happiness.

Herbert Vogel, a postal worker in New York City, and his librarian wife, Dorothy, illustrate this point. Devoted to contemporary art of the 1950s and 1960s, they bought pieces by struggling artists and helped them jump-start their careers. Many of these artists are now world-renowned and their early works are worth millions. On their meager salaries, the Vogels accumulated a massive and valuable art collection. They could do it because they loved art and felt it was their calling to be collectors.

The Vogels' story illustrates another important point about *B'shert.* Just as a rainbow cannot appear without rain, the Vogels' happiness was mingled with regret because they never wanted to part with a single work of art.

"Each piece is like one of our children," Mrs. Vogel once said. "When we had no more room, we had to find a suitable place for this 'family' of ours to live." With much anguish, they eventually donated all but a few pieces to the National Gallery of Art in Washington, D.C. so that others could enjoy their collection.

Every joy always includes a small measure of regret. Think of parents who want only the best for their children and work hard to make them into independent adults. If they are successful, their joy is troubled by the pain of realizing that their kids don't really need them any longer. Like the Olympic athlete who trains, sacrifices, achieves a goal and then finds that the only thing that survives are memories, we must adjust our life path as circumstances change. This is why the ancients teach that all of us have more than one predestined path to walk in our lives. As we meet our goals, we must continually adjust and choose new directions.

Depending on God's Intervention May Obscure Divine Gifts

Small, seemingly apparent "accidents" of fate aren't accidents at all. What often seems like good fortune is frequently the result of studied alertness over a long period of time. Coincidences, according to the ancients, are part of the *visioning* that is a major element of a spiritual life. They believed that opportunities multiply when they are seized and that they die when they are neglected. As Louis Pasteur said, "Chance favors the prepared mind."

We can lose our way just as much by depending too much on God's intervention. A wonderful example is the story of a poor man whose house was directly in the path of an approaching flood. A police car was dispatched to save the man before the flood waters began to rise, but the man sent the police car back. "I have put my trust in the Lord. The Lord will save me. That is what I'm awaiting."

As the waters rose, a boat was sent to bring the man to safety. The man sent the rowboat away with the words: "I have put my trust in the Lord. The Lord will save me. That is what I'm awaiting."

Finally, a helicopter was sent after the man had climbed on his roof to avoid the rising water. Clinging to his chimney, the man sent the rescuers away: "I have put my trust in the Lord. The Lord will save me. That is what I'm awaiting."

After the man drowned, he arrived at the pearly gates and demanded to know why his maker had not intervened to save him. "Listen," God said. "I sent a car, a boat and a helicopter. What more could I do?"

God's help doesn't necessarily come in a dramatic way. It need not be a parting of the sea or the winning of a lottery jackpot. If we spend our energies expecting such assistance, we may miss the small gifts from God, such as a radio interview about underprivileged kids and baseball.

Charting Our Map to Happiness

How can we create and maintain our own road map to happiness? The most prevalent impediment to finding joy is that most of us lack such a map. We would certainly not embark on any other trip without an itinerary. Sailors, for instance do not go to sea without navigational charts and a sailing plan. But most of us begin each day with little idea of where we want to go, much less how we plan to get there.

The ancients believed that to find joy we must:

- Write down what brings us joy and happiness. Figure out whether it's a whim or if it is truly what we want more than anything else in life.

- Create a plan every day that lets us include in our daily lives as much as possible of what makes us happy.

- As we live that plan, our *B'shert* will emerge because we will be sensitized to the opportunities that await us. There may be times when we don't really know what we're made to do, but the wonderful mystery of life lies in our willingness to discover it.

- Once we spot an opportunity, we must seize it, and adjust our course. Like a pilot, we have to understand that the wrong wind, a miscalculation, a misunderstanding or a missed communication can throw us off line.

By choosing something that will make us happy and creating a plan to make it happen in our lives, we not only bring joy to ourselves, but help create positive energy in the universe that was not there before. The new energy produces a spiritual center within us which connects us to the divine.

This is akin to walking into a holy place and focusing on the awe that is sensed. Knowing that we are in a special place we touch and see everything differently. The Kabbalists believed that this feeling arose from the feminine side of God and brought us in touch with the sensitive side of ourselves. It is what the ancients called the very presence of God in our lives, or the *Shechinah*.

In other words, by brightening the lives of others with our search for joy, our happiness becomes a holiness that gives us a spiritual center and enhances everything around us.

Exercises for the Soul

Monday
Think about a way to do what you love and have it benefit others. For example, if you love to act, you might join a public theater company in your community—or form one.

Tuesday
Take your project idea and examine what is necessary in time, effort and resources for it to become a reality. If you do it correctly, this project might become more important than your livelihood, so spend the time and the effort to make this study complete.

Wednesday
Envision yourself doing this project. Imagine yourself making mistakes and having fun. Imagine the

details. For example, if you are an aspiring actor, see yourself reading the script and then walking into your first audition.

Thursday Go to a library or bookstore and get two books or magazines that will give you more information about aspects of your project or help you contact others who might be involved in similar efforts.

Friday Make your initial "to-do" list. Plan the time that you'll need each day to work on it.

Saturday Tell one person whom you trust about your plan. Consider their opinions and ideas.

Sunday To commit yourself entirely to the project, do something that will make it almost impossible to give it up. Write a letter to someone far away or someone you haven't seen in some time and describe your plan to them. Understand that all you have done so far is go through a planning process. In the weeks and months to come, you will have to do the hard work of making your project a reality.

CHAPTER 8

GETTING YOUR ATTITUDE ADJUSTED

Becoming connected to a process that leads to spiritual happiness is a matter of attitude and altitude. A bad attitude doesn't provide sufficient altitude to lift us above the mundane. A good one will. But how can we grab it in the first place, and then how do we hold on while we make our way up?

The mystics believed that to succeed against the forces of hopelessness and gloom, a person who wants happiness must first develop a mental armor. The world is filled with pain, problems and misleading information. Faced properly all these can sharpen our instincts. If life were too easy, there would be no personal fulfillment when we meet and overcome a challenge.

In fact, if we had all the answers, what would we strive toward? Indeed, overcoming fear and developing mental toughness is very much a matter of acquiring enough information to remove doubt, anxiety or fear.

Not long ago, a Polish newspaper reported the harrowing voyage of the freighter *Phenian*. During heavy seas in the Atlantic Ocean, mysterious voices began calling from the cargo hold below deck. At first, the crew thought that it was the wind playing tricks with their ears. But even when the winds briefly became calm the voices still rose from below with each wave that tossed the ship from side to side. Convinced the ship was bewitched by demons, the sailors panicked. Some even suggested abandoning ship.

The captain stayed calm and tried to decipher the ghostly voices. Finally, he called the crew together and brought them to the place in the hold that was the source of the sounds. He took an ax and hacked at a cargo crate, splitting it apart in front of his astonished crew. Out poured hundreds of dolls, each crying "Mama," every time a wave rocked the ship and tipped them from side to side.

Fear of the unknown had panicked these hardened sailors. But information gave them the courage to continue on their voyage, strengthening them against paranoia and making them more willing to take risks in the future. Willingness to take such risks is essential to changing our attitude toward life.

According to a Yiddish proverb, "A ship in a harbor is always safe. But that's not what a ship is built for." Joy is not possible if we stay too close to home and play life too safe. It is not achieved by watching television all day or by taking drugs to dull our senses. Happiness is not an escape. It is just the opposite. It is possible only when we make up our minds that we are willing to take risks.

Repairing the Fragments of Our Lives

A resilient, risk-taking attitude does not, on its own, create a good attitude. Far from it. Just as a body must be physically trained to compete in sports, so too must the mind be toughened before it can embark on any spiritual journey. No one ever became a tennis star, for example, by only developing stamina and muscle strength. Skills and strategy must be built into a well-trained body to create a winner. The same applies to your attitude.

To understand how to develop the proper attitude, it is essential to recall the basic business of the mystic: Fixing a broken world and making it whole. Spiritual faith is enhanced by repairing the broken fragments of our own lives, then noticing what's broken in the larger world and trying to repair that.

To build a good attitude, identify your interests.

That, in turn, will lead to excitement.

Close behind will be involvement.

That will create understanding.

That's the key to ideas that can repair a small corner of the world.

Identifying interests can be a complex business. Too often, we choose interests that appeal to a friend, a relative or an employer, instead of searching for what satisfies *us*. It is too easy to let people we love or need make our choices for us or push us toward their notions of what we should care about. What parent doesn't try to steer his or her child toward certain careers or hobbies? How many times do we go to a movie just because someone else wants to go? How often do we make a menu choice because we heard someone say it was worthwhile? How often have we given up on things in which we believed because someone considered them poor ideas?

It is one thing to use another person's expertise to make our own choices, but letting that expertise dictate what we do almost always results in an unsatisfying outcome. It is fine, of course, to make another person happy by sometimes pleasing them. But remember that no one can choose your interests for you. If you are not faithful to your own interests and proclivities, you cannot move to the next step in the process and acquire excitement.

A young man I know wanted to become an entrepreneur during the summer after his high school graduation. His concept was to purchase a pushcart from which he would sell brownies baked by an uncle who was in the restaurant business.

His father was thrilled by his son's sense of enterprise. But, he suggested, not everybody would want brownies and the market might be too limited. Perhaps the cart could sell another line of desserts? "A lot of your uncle's customers get ice cream with their brownies," the father said. "Why not sell ice cream?"

The son protested: "I just want to sell brownies. Keeping ice cream frozen will be complicated."

The father dismissed his son's concerns: "All you need is the right kind of cart."

"But I don't know where to get a cart like that," the son said.

"Well, let's find out," the father countered. "I'll make a

few calls." As soon as the father began calling people he knew in the food business, the son tried to think of other alternatives for summer employment.

The father soon found a bicycle-propelled ice cream cart, discovered where to buy wholesale ice cream, worked out how much ice cream to buy each week and the flavors and varieties that would be popular. He even talked with the Board of Health and with lawyers and accountants. Before long, he had everything in place that the son would need for a successful ice cream and brownie business.

Satisfied that his son was now well on his way, the father went back to his own trade. After a week, the father visited his son at the proposed ice cream route, only to discover the boy was nowhere to be found. He called his son at home and discovered that the cart had not even been painted yet for the planned refurbishing. "My friend promised he'd paint it this weekend," his son said in a sleepy voice.

The rest of the summer went much the same way. Many mornings, the father called home only to find his son just waking up.

"It was cloudy when I woke up earlier," the young man explained. "Who buys ice cream when it's cloudy?"

On July Fourth, the father found his son watching fireworks in the middle of a crowded street. "You should have your cart here," the father said. "You could have sold out on a hot night like tonight." The son shrugged. "Then I'd miss the fireworks."

The father naturally wanted to help his son, but his mistake was in taking over his son's idea. Once that happened, the business "belonged" to his father.

Excitement Is Genuine if the Interest Is Genuine

Moving from interest to excitement can be relatively seamless if the interest is truly ours. One sign that we are focusing on something that makes sense to us is how much our excitement spills over to other aspects of our lives. A hard-driving businessman may be excited by the deal-making process. To him, earning money is not really the point. The fun is in the tumult and the action: It is all about making the deal. Another man may focus on something as peripheral to his work as his next round of golf, playing and replaying different holes on varied courses in his mind while resting or traveling to work. He may attribute his success in business to his preoccupation with golf: "I work hard so that I can afford to play at the best courses in the world."

Once we are "turned on" by our interests, we need to keep the excitement going to the next level. Most of us will never have the luxury of being able to do what excites us every waking hour. In view of that, the ancients devised a technique to achieve a sense of ongoing excitement that requires us to spend some time doing the exciting activity and a lot of time thinking about it. By spending, say, ten percent of our day doing what excites us and 60 percent of our day looking forward to the next day's ten percent, we create a sense of perpetual motion, a sense of being enveloped by the positive energy of excitement.

Being caught up in our excitement moves us easily to being involved. How do we know if we're involved? We're involved if we can be alone with ourselves, if we can become totally immersed in our excitement, although that

120

doesn't mean we are obsessed with it. The level of involvement demonstrated by our Type A businessman and deal-maker is no greater than that shown by the proprietor of the book store in a Vermont town where this sign on the front door greets visitors:

"We're open Monday through Saturday at 9 a.m. Occasionally, if it's a really nice day, we open as early as 8:30. But some days, especially if it is raining, we don't open until 11 a.m. We close about 5 p.m. or 5:30. Occasionally, we close at 4:30, especially when the world seems dreary."

Everyone is different. Some people can extract bits of excitement from a number of places. Others are interested in just one thing. To the mystical mind, there is nothing wrong with either approach. What matters is not the goal as much as the process to achieve it. Understanding grows when our involvement in this process lifts us out of self-absorption. Then, our interests turn us into interesting people with moments of self-understanding.

These moments of perception are the gateway to the mystical place that lets us repair our lives so that we can help repair the world around us. That place is transcendent, almost magical. Rescue workers, for example, in the midst of tiring and emotionally wrenching work, surrounded by pain and death, experience fulfillment and meaning. Psychological studies have shown that being totally involved in the work of saving lives makes them almost immune from depression and fear. It lets them rise above concerns for their own safety and do things that under normal circumstances would be physically or mentally impossible.

These moments transcend time and space. When we become so totally immersed in what we're doing, the experience takes on a life of its own and is so riveting that we want to encounter it over and over again. It is then that we have achieved something truly mystical.

The ability to create these transcendent moments, which so often are the key to professional and personal success, often gets hindered by that very success. In college, for example, some of the keenest minds I knew were bound for medical school. Years later, most of those minds had seemed to shrivel up, often focusing only on their own field. At a gathering of doctors and non-doctors, when the conversation switched to other subjects, they would become visibly bored, maybe leaving the room to continue the conversation elsewhere.

When I asked these doctors if they were happy with their work, many said they were not. There were two exceptions. One doctor had just returned from Somalia, where he had served with volunteers trying to save thousands from starvation. The second had studied the violin as a youngster and was now involved in a quartet. Both spoke about many things besides medicine; both seemed interested in everyone around them. When asked if they were happy, the answer was immediate and enthusiastic: "Yes."

Weaving Joyous Moments into Daily Life

No matter what our work may be, we can experience moments of transcendent joy during our entire life, if that life is filled with what interests, excites and involves us and brings a personal understanding of ourselves that raises us to a mystical level of joy. That joy need not be intense and distracting. It need not set us apart from the day-to-day process of living. We can—and we should—weave those moments into the normal fabric of our lives.

Richard, for example, is an electrician by day, a scholar in a local university by night and an example of how to live that sort of seemingly disparate life. He has three master's degrees, a doctorate and a law degree. One might wonder: Why doesn't he figure out what he wants to do? Richard's answer is simple: "I am doing exactly what I want to do, day and night. When I work, the day seems to fly by. Everything feels right with each new project. Then at night, I go to a place where I feel at home, where there are new things to learn and where ideas flow freely."

What happens when our lives are altered by powerful negative changes? Overcoming adversity and building mental toughness is one thing, but certain events in life will pierce even the toughest armor. Mystics believe that even life's most painful times are essential for creating the sensibility and sensitivity to be happy.

People whose long-time spouses, for instance, have died may react in one of two ways. Those who lock themselves away from the world are always the ones who had no lives of their own before their spouses died. They had stripped themselves of purpose years before they found themselves alone. Those who could still experience joy after their loss suffered no less than the others. After mourning, they could still enjoy life again, take chances again and find an interest and develop an excitement and involvement that led to understanding and, eventually, spiritual joy.

Of course, all of us go through a mourning period. Our hearts and spirits shut down. The ancients believed that this reaction was natural, even that it was a blessing. The Jewish period of intense mourning, called *Shiva,* which is followed by a less intense period, *Shloshim,* and, finally, a more subdued mourning for a year, teaches that we can only get over loss little by little, taking small steps that repair our souls. We can rise above our loss if we focus our skills and intelligence on repairing our small corners of the world.

Exercises for the Soul

Monday	If you could choose your interests, regardless of what others might say or think about them, what would you select? Write these down.
Tuesday	If you had to select interests based on what others expect of you, what would they be? Write these down.
Wednesday	What excites you? What gets your blood circulating and your mind focused? Make a list of these.

Thursday	Identify the proudest moments of your life. Write them down.
Friday	Identify what you would like to learn about or do during the next two years. Write them down.
Saturday	Compare these various lists that you compiled from Monday to Friday. Are there patterns or common elements? Are the items on your Wednesday and Thursday lists more closely related to the Monday or the Tuesday list of interests?
Sunday	Use the insights you gained from Saturday's exercise to develop a one-page plan that links your interests (Monday's list) more closely to your life. Can you use these interests to repair a small part of *your* world?

CHAPTER 9

MAKING SENSE, NOT EXCUSES

Among life's many choices, few will as profoundly affect our happiness as this: When we are presented with an opportunity, do we take a risk? Or do we make an excuse?

Most of us, because of fear or laziness, prefer excuses at every turn. To mystics, an occasional excuse is okay. It gives us a needed breather from the hard work of building our lives and creating happiness. But when our excuses become a habitual cop-out, our souls begin to wither. That's why the ancient Jewish texts warn us about life's three most dangerous excuses:

"I'll be happy when I acquire _____" *(fill in the blank with an object, amount of money or some goal).*

"I don't have the time to _____" *(fill in the blank with some activity that would make you happy).*

"I would be happy or successful if other people didn't hold me back because of my _____" (*fill in the blank with your ethnicity, race, personality trait, economic class or another convenient personal quality that can't be changed and that makes you a "victim"*).

These excuses of opportunity, time and paranoia harm our souls because they are easy for us to make and easy for others to accept. Over time, they can define how we live day-to-day, and lock us into lethargy and misery.

Stop Feeling Sorry for Yourself

If we wait for the "right opportunity" to present itself, it is likely that our happiness, in terms a dice gambler would find familiar, is based on the "come." If something will happen, only then will happiness arrive. There's the child who is certain that joy can come only by owning a bike or a certain piece of clothing. Or the woman who is certain that the only way she will find happiness is by marrying the man of her dreams. Or the man who is convinced that he will only be happy when he finally retires from work that has made him miserable. Or the couple which is convinced that the only way to insure happiness is by accumulating enough money, with "enough" being either undefined or an ever-expanding amount.

Jewish mystics believed that setting goals and waiting for opportunities is a powerful tool. Yet, the tendency to wait for something else to happen before focusing on what's good about our lives is dangerous and usually unrewarding.

The bicycle will not be a panacea for the child. The single person who is unhappy is likely to make two people miserable in marriage. Retirement and wealth are both among life's potential pleasures, but they are just means to an end.

Many of us believe that we are not good enough to enjoy who we are or what we're doing. Whenever a chance for happiness comes close, some automatic reflex jerks us back to our self-doubts. We can almost hear ourselves saying: "You don't deserve this happiness because you haven't yet _____ (*fill in the blank*)!" The mystics call the chaotic, ambivalent push-and-pull of the universe *tzimtzum*. When we succeed, yet still feel terrible inside, we internalize our ambivalence and recreate *tzimtzum* in our souls.

This confusion, which makes us feel bad when we should feel great, eventually leads to self-contempt. We ask ourselves, "Who do you think you are?" We feel unworthy to receive anything good. So, rather than take the chance of enjoying a potential reward, we put our whole world on hold by making an excuse.

Instead of pinning our hopes on what might come, the common sense response to counteract the negative effect of our *tzimtzum* is to focus on things that we can achieve or control.

Consider Ginny, a woman who had always thought of herself as totally average. Since she was a small girl, her parents had encouraged her to look forward to marriage and motherhood. After she graduated from high school, her family assured her that she would soon find the "right" boy. She was convinced that her life would really begin once she was married. While majoring in education at college, she minored in marriage planning: The details of the bridal showers, the wedding ceremony, the reception, the honeymoon, the first apartment, the house, even the two kids she would have after three years of wedded bliss.

Her college professors noticed her writing talent. One even offered her a scholarship to a prestigious summer writer's workshop. Ginny turned it down because, while she did indeed love to write, she hoped to find a different sort of love that summer. So she got a job as a counselor in a Wisconsin camp because a boy she hoped to get to know better would be working there, too.

The scholarship went to another woman who, though talented, was not Ginny's equal as a writer. Eight years have now passed and Ginny is still not married. But the woman who attended the conference works for a national magazine, a job she obtained because of the connections she made at the writer's workshop that Ginny passed up. The woman did invite Ginny to her wedding to another writer, a young man she met at the summer workshop.

Ginny is now miserable. Her friends have told her that she should get a graduate degree in writing or maybe be a freelance writer. But Ginny wants to do nothing that would take time away from her social life because she is convinced that the man of her dreams is just a dinner party away.

Seize Opportunities—or They'll Be Wasted

Ginny's story may be unique. But the substance of it—postponing her happiness while waiting for some future opportunity—is common to many of us. We can focus so much on objectives over which we have no control that we may overlook opportunities within our reach.

An Armenian fable tells of a young man who was so devastated by his poverty and despair that he decided to find the Messiah and ask how to discover true happiness.

While looking for the Messiah, he met an emaciated wolf. "Where are you going, my young friend?"

"To find the Messiah," our young man said. "I am going to ask him what should be my true destiny. Life until now has been terrible. I work hard all day, but I am still poor. I have no wife and I'm lonely. If this is my fate and all I can expect then I will accept it and be happy with it. If this is not the way it should be, then how can I change my destiny?"

"Well, my friend," said the wolf, "if you find the Messiah would you ask him one question for me? Ask the Holy One how I can relieve myself from the hunger I feel."

The man assured the wolf he would not forget the question and went on his way. Soon he came upon a beautiful, but sad, young woman who asked where he was bound. When he explained his mission, the woman asked, "My handsome young friend, would you ask the Holy One why a woman who everyone says is so pretty and well-to-do has not found a man who will love her and be part of her life?"

The man promised the beautiful maiden that he would ask her question and went on his way.

By a stream, the man came upon a tree that was green on one side and dying on the other. "Young man," the tree said, "where are you going in such a hurry?" The fellow told his story to the tree, who pleaded that he ask "why a tree that is right next to a lovely stream is dying from thirst?"

Promising that the question would be asked, the man continued with his quest.

Eventually, he came upon the Messiah standing on a mountaintop surveying the world. "Oh, Holy One," the young man said. "I have come a long way to ask you my question."

"Because of your persistence and your youth, I shall give you your answer," said the Messiah. "Despair is not supposed to be your destiny. If you are wise, all you have to do to find your happiness is to take advantage of the luck that you shall find in your world. That is your destiny."

The young man then asked questions for the tree, the maiden and the fox, and was given their answers, as well.

The elated young man then re-traced his steps. "Where are you going in such a hurry, my young friend?" asked the tree.

"The Messiah told me that all I have to do is find my luck, and then I shall be happy."

"Forgive me for slowing you down, but did you ask about my problem?" the tree wondered.

"Oh yes. The Messiah told me that when you were just a sapling, a rich man buried a huge treasure chest filled with gold coins under your branches. The man died and never told a soul where his fortune could be found. Now that you have grown, the treasure has gotten in the way of your roots. All that needs to be done for your branches to have green leaves again is for someone to dig up the treasure."

"So dig up the treasure. You shall be rich beyond your wildest dreams, and I shall grow and be green."

"Oh, no," the young man said as he ran down the road. "I couldn't do that. I'm in too much of a hurry. I have to find my luck. That is my true destiny and only that shall bring me happiness."

And he left the tree to die by the stream.

As he approached the maiden, she rushed to greet him. He told her of his good news and then gave her the answer to her question: "You will meet a young man who will come from afar. You shall ask him to be yours, and, if he is wise, he will accept and join you. Then the two of you will live happily ever after."

The woman smiled. "So, my young friend, be mine and we will live a wonderful life together."

"Oh, no," said the young man. "Although you are very beautiful, I am in too much of a hurry. You see, I have to find my luck, because that is my true destiny. Only that shall bring me happiness."

Finally, the young man met the wolf.

"The Messiah said that one fine day you shall encounter a foolish man who has no idea what he's missed in his life," the young man said. "When he comes your way, you will know what to do with him, and you will not be hungry for many days."

"Well," the wolf said with a smile, "I must be the luckiest wolf in all the world, because I have discovered my destiny." At that moment, the young man's adventure—and the wolf's hunger—came to an abrupt end.

The wolf understood the relationship between happiness and seizing an opportunity, rather than waiting for one. And the young man understood nothing.

Take Control Over Your Time

"I don't have the time."

How often in our lives have we heard this from people explaining their lack of accomplishment or motivation? How often have those words left our own lips? Whether we believe we have too little time or too much, this excuse effectively snuffs out our chances for happiness.

Folklore and wisdom from many sources make this point. Abraham Lincoln, for example, once said: "Things may come to those who wait, but only the things that have been left behind by those who have already been there."

And a medieval Jewish story tells of Satan gathering all his assistants to discuss the most effective way to destroy the meaning of people's lives. One helper suggested, "Tell them there is no God." Another offered, "Tell them that there is no judgment for sin and they need not worry." A third said, "Tell them that their sins are so huge that they will never be forgiven." Finally, Satan stepped in and suggested, "We should simply tell them to relax because they have all the time in the world."

For me, an executive named Fred disproved the notion that there's not enough time to do what we really care about. The devil would have a tough time with him, because Fred squeezes every moment for its full potential.

Fred runs a multi-national corporation. Every day, he wakes up early because he's made up his mind that exercise is important. You see, his former business partner, who demanded to be addressed formally as Mr. Sunn, once told him that he never had enough time to exercise. Fred feels that it makes his day more vibrant whenever he does his 30 minutes on the treadmill, in part because Mr. Sunn never had the time. His partner always said that he would get around to doing the things he missed once he retired. When Fred eventually bought out Mr. Sunn's interest in the business, Mr. Sunn and his wife moved into the house of their dreams in a warmer climate, armed with a list of the things that they had put off in their lives. Two months later, Mr. Sunn had a massive stroke and was totally incapacitated for four years before he died.

After his former partner's stroke, Fred didn't cut back on his 14-hour work days, but he did decide not to wait until retirement to live his life. Each day, he picks one thing that he will read or do for an hour that he might have put off until his retirement. Whether Fred is in town or on a business trip, he devotes one night each week to a play, a movie or a lecture that has nothing to do with his business. One week of the year, Fred goes on a trip that he might have saved for his retirement.

We can all find ways to make ourselves too busy for those things or people that make us most happy. Some of us are even convinced that the people who mean the most to us will understand that work comes first. But as a Hungarian proverb advises: "If you want more time, don't look for it. Make it."

We can adopt a number of practical strategies to make better use of our time. If you think you don't have time to read books, you can listen to audio tapes while driving or doing housework or exercise. When you feel exhausted and just want to drop in front of the television, you can try to get interested in something before boredom eats away your soul. Enroll in nighttime or weekend continuing education classes at a college or university. Sign up at a sports league, a clinic or a recreational club. And surely a charity could benefit, just one night per week, from your skills.

Don't Be a "Victim" and Blame Others for Your Unhappiness

Paranoia is a powerful rationalizing tool. It encourages us to give up before we have even begun. By convincing us that people loathe us, paranoid fears are plausible because discrimination is, indeed, a fact of life. Like a comfortable old shirt or a bowl of chicken soup when we are feeling down, it comforts us and conveniently explains our failures: "I knew those people had it in for me because I'm _____ (fill in the blank)." The role of victim is the easiest part for us to play in life because it seems that so many of us were born to play it.

We would be naive to believe that we don't have enemies because we have a different faith, skin color or nationality. We've all heard that "even paranoids have real enemies." This is true. It's just as true, though, that without some degree of trust we will never have a meaningful degree of happiness. The African-American who is convinced that every white person is the enemy and that her every effort to succeed is blocked by racists is certainly bound to fail. The Jew who gives up on corporate life because he believes non-Jews will thwart his every career advancement is not a victim of hate, but of self-doubt. The woman who refuses to apply for a challenging job because she assumes that the man doing the hiring is sexist limits her professional options and weakens her self-esteem.

There *are* racists, misogynists and anti-Semites in this world. But many more only want the best for themselves, their organizations and us. When we don't give people a chance, we don't give ourselves a chance.

Nat is that way. He believes that every time he gets into a position to make something of himself, an anti-Semite will stop him. He's a talented systems analyst, but he hasn't had a promotion in four years. Although he gets very high grades on his work, his superiors feel that Nat has a bad attitude toward them and his work. Nat, of course, doesn't see it that way. He's convinced that someone on his management team has it in for him. Even though two of the ten supervisors who can affect his career are Jewish, Nat calls them "Jewish Uncle Toms." He doesn't believe that his open contempt for his bosses has anything to do with his lack of advancement: "They're terrified that if one Jew who isn't afraid of them gets promoted, more Jews will come." Yet, several years ago when he attempted to get a position with an Israeli computer firm, he wasn't hired because, he said, he was an American.

Even in the face of genuine discrimination, life can present innumerable opportunities to us to conquer petty hatred for those of us who don't use it as an excuse. For example, an African-American, Colin Powell, whose parents emigrated from the West Indies to the United States, grew up not only to hold the highest rank in the world's most powerful military, but also to help lead his country to victory in the Persian Gulf War.

"Making Sense" Instead of Excuses
Makes Us Succeed

The Powells of this world will tell us that anyone can over-come perceived disadvantage. There may be times to walk away rather than challenge real hatred and discrimination. In most cases, though, adopting a positive viewpoint will allay prejudice and prevent us from falling victim to life's excuses.

This is called "making sense."

Let's illustrate how to make sense of things by examin-ing how people react to losing a wallet. One type of person will play the victim and look for someone to blame. They will go to pieces wondering what will happen to them now that they don't have their driver's license, the family pic-tures and the credit cards. They will rant and rave about the injustice of it, how these things always happen to them.

The more successful person understands that wallets get lost, that "stuff happens." Before this person gets angry they take command of the situation by beginning the process of replacing what was lost and getting on with life. They make sense of the situation, which is the necessary first step to getting control of feelings and putting loss into perspective.

In doing so, they eliminate dependence on excuses.

Making sense instead of excuses is a courageous thing to do, even if it just means dealing with losing a wallet in-stead of being angered by it. In situations of more significance to our lives, it takes real guts to make sense of things. This courage, the mystics argue, is the mysterious ingredient of a happy soul. They tell us to take a good look at our lives without excuses and to have the will to make sense of the things that interfere with our happiness.

A spiritual state of happiness is assured even if the change proves to be ill-advised in the end. Courageous decisions always lead to rewarding trips, even if the final destination is not one we had planned. Who knows, we might be lucky and even end up in _____ *(fill in the blank)*.

Exercises for the Soul

Monday	Identify the obstacles you think stand in the way of your happiness. Complete the statement, "I'd be happier if...."
Tuesday	Ask two people you love and trust to identify the obstacles in the way of your happiness. Ask them to finish the statement, "You'd be happier if...."
Wednesday	In an ideal world, how could you overcome the least formidable of these obstacles?
Thursday	Write a half-page plan to overcome the obstacles that keep you from moving toward your happiness.
Friday	Identify two activities in your life that regularly waste your time. Write a half-page plan to eliminate one

of them from your life.

Saturday: Reflect on the notion of time. What is it? How do you use it? Are you busy doing things that are meaningful to you? Do you know anyone who seems to use time effectively? Call and ask that person for their "secret."

Sunday Write down five facts to support the statement, "People are against me because of my race, color, religion or another aspect of my life I cannot control." Then write down five things that support the statement, "I know people are not against me in any organized way because of what I've achieved in my life."

CHAPTER 10

THE POWER OF "NO"

To be happy, we must *no* ourselves.

That's right. This simple word spoken at the appropriate times in our lives can be a potent mantra in our mystical arsenal. It can vanquish anxieties, beat back depression and overpower addictions. Like a valuable tactical weapon, we can use it with precision and discretion to:

- Control our bad habits before they control us.
- Fight off the inertia that makes us want to give up on ourselves and our lives when things go wrong.

Consider Hildy, a compulsive eater who hated every morsel of food she put to her lips. The only thing she hated more was herself for not being able to suppress her urge to eat. Beneath the 100 pounds of her extra weight was a brilliant woman with a steel-trap mind and a quick wit.

"I just can't stop eating," she said. "Every diet I tried

was a failure and made me feel like a failure."

That failure led to complacency. And complacency led to a belief that her eating problem was a lost cause. "Each time I went on a diet, I got nervous and hungrier. And some automatic eating response kept clicking itself on. Hungry or not, I ate. Eventually, I just figured, why bother? If this was something I couldn't deal with, why even try?

"Then, I saw Annie for the first time in years. She was another fat girl. I disliked her because every time I saw her, I saw myself. This time, I saw something more, or actually something less: 130 pounds less.

"This girl was fat all of her life. She was dumb as a post. She had absolutely nothing going for her. Yet she had managed to slim down to a very presentable size. My competitive urge took over. I just had to know how she had done it. So I asked her for her secret."

Hildy tried her friend's secret. She placed a loose fitting rubber band around her wrist, and, every time she thought about food, she would say one word loud and clear, "No," and then snap the rubber band. If she began to eat when she wasn't hungry, she said, "No," and snapped herself with the rubber band. Whenever she thought about eating food not on her diet, she snapped the rubber band and said, "No!"

In 12 months, Hildy lost her extra weight. And she kept it off. The rubber band had freed her from self-loathing by teaching that she had the power to control her negative impulses. The word "no" had opened up opportunities to say "yes" to a happy life.

Too Many "No's" Are Dangerous

Learning to use "No" as an effective tool is tough. Think about how much easier it is to say "yes" to a child who has asked for a toy. Isn't it easier to eat a bit more than we should or to appease our lazy urges and end an exercise session early or skip it entirely?

In contrast, isn't it also sometimes easier once we start saying "no" to a child to use that response to every request? How many family tragedies were created by the parent who never said anything *except* "no," who used this powerful weapon injudiciously and raised a child who was ill-equipped to understand proportion and boundaries?

Many of us have heard stories about parents and their child who walked away from one another because the child rebelled against their frequent and inappropriate prohibitions. Sandra, for instance, grew up in a politically conservative home where she received a strong Jewish religious education. The affluent parents provided their daughter with all sorts of travel and fine possessions. All three would say that there was real love in their home when Sandra was growing up.

Throughout her childhood, Sandra bent her will to her parents' unyielding rules.

Through high school, Sandra was the obedient daughter. She showed real aptitude for marine biology, but her parents refused to send her to an ocean science camp. Who knew what kind of people go to a camp like that? Instead, she went to the same camp that many of her friends from synagogue attended year after year. When it was time to select a college, her parents refused to send her to a school in California with a prestigious marine sciences program. Instead, they steered her to a good school closer to home that matched their needs better than their daughter's.

Because she had no sense of how to set her own limits, Sandra said "yes" to everything while she was in college, including alcohol, drugs, promiscuous sex and an errant spiritual journey through pop psychology and New Age mysticism.

Sandra's parents were dismayed. "'You shouldn't do that,'" Sandra recalls her parents telling her. "That's all they ever said when they saw me. So, I stopped going home. When I told them I was getting married, the first question they asked was whether my fiancé was Jewish. He wasn't, and they said I couldn't marry him. Well, of course, I did, and they did not attend the wedding."

Sandra now does research on aquatic life in the Great Lakes. She reconciled with her parents after the birth of her first child. Still, she regrets the years of pain she and her parents endured because she was always told "no" rather than taught when and how to say "no" herself. And her parents regret that she considered them inflexible ogres rather than loving adults with the experience and wisdom to know the "right" thing to do.

Use Discipline Sparingly and Wisely—and Use Trust

Learning an adult self-discipline is called "strength" or *Gevurah* by the Kabbalists. It is what lets us control that part of us that never matures, our childish emotions and passions that can dominate. This infant inside of us can make us cranky or willful or slaves to a habit or an addiction. It can make us go in unpredictable directions and it feels as if there's a two-year-old child at the controls. When there's a kid driving, there's no way we can experience the joy intended for us.

Mystics believe that the demon we should most fear is not some outside power that can compel us to do its bidding. They want us to be on the alert for the small gremlin inside that demands total submission by coercing us to think that we have no options. It is this untrusting child, fearful of moving on and growing up that is most dangerous.

Essential to practical spirituality is an ability to trust. Trust puts an adult in the driver's seat. It gives us the ability to control ourselves. With trust, we know when it's all right to stop or when it's appropriate to persist when persistence is needed.

Habits, passions, addictions and overindulgence all have the capacity to control and rule our lives. When that happens, our senses dull and we become self-absorbed. The widow who is so depressed that she can't leave her home for months is not mourning anyone but herself. The man addicted to prescription drugs and totally engrossed in meeting his own needs is spiritually dead.

Say "No" to Fear and Meet New Challenges

The ancients were convinced that every habit leads to self-absorption. That leads to constant self-gratification. And that, in turn, leads to unfulfilled dreams and unrealistic goals.

Once that occurs, we are certain life has no meaning and that we are not good enough to control our own lives.

The person with an addiction who feels it cannot be broken, or the one who doesn't finish a critical project, or those who don't show up for defining events in their lives are all ruled by fear. They are afraid of failure, of success, of criticism, of adulation, of growing up. This is a state in which we all find ourselves at some point in our lives. When the gremlin inside takes control, we must control it. The only way to do so is by saying "no" to fear, to procrastination, to hopelessness. What, after all, is the alternative?

An old tale tells of a frog who slipped into a wagon rut while crossing a road. His friends gathered around and tried to help him jump out, but the rut was deep and the mud very soft. Fellow frogs gave him directions and advice. Others offered emotional support.

"You can do it," they said. "You've got what it takes."

Then they heard a wagon approaching and saw that its wheels were traveling in the very same rut that imprisoned their friend. They all scattered, because they couldn't bring themselves to watch what they were certain would happen when the wagon reached their pal. Some cried; others closed their eyes. Everyone tried not to think about the frog flattened in that deep, muddy rut.

The next day they were shocked when they saw their friend hopping across the meadow.

"That rut was too deep and too muddy for you to escape. How did you do it?" they asked in amazement.

The frog answered matter-of-factly: "All I know is that I had to do it, so I found a way to do it."

If our hero the frog were Jewish, he might have quoted the Yiddish proverb that says: "When you must, you will." If he were a Kabbalist, he might have realized his *Gevurah,* his real strength, and added: When you *no,* you can.

Exercises for the Soul

Monday   Ask a few friends which of your habits or compulsions they don't like. For example, are you chronically late? Do you overeat? Do you drink excessively? Do you watch too much television?

Tuesday   Ask yourself the same question you asked your friends yesterday.

Wednesday   List the negative habits that you and your friends agree you have.

Thursday   Concentrate on breaking the least formidable habit for just one day. Say "no" to yourself each time this habit surfaces.

Friday   Concentrate on breaking the most formidable habit for just one day. If you are a smoker, for example, quit for the day.

Saturday   Reward yourself for your two days of success by giving yourself a special, non-habitual reward. Buy yourself a rose. Treat yourself to a movie. Take yourself out to a ball game. You pick that special treat that means something to you.

Sunday   List all the things in your life that you wanted to do, but haven't done, such as writing a book, learning how to play the piano or traveling to Hawaii. Group them into two categories: Easy to do; difficult to do. Do the easy ones first. Then go for the big ones.

CHAPTER 11

BE MYSTICAL. BE HAPPY.

Mysticism and practical spirituality are not just harmless philosophical playthings. Traditional scholars treated the subject not only with great respect, but with tremendous caution. They strictly limited Kabbalah study to married men over the age of 40. Some teachers even required the equivalent of a graduate degree in Jewish studies before they let anyone open a book on mystical thought. Stories abound of defiant young men who ignored their elders' warnings and dabbled in the mysteries of the soul. Their reward was madness or death.

Practitioners of mystical Judaism weren't trying to maintain the value of their knowledge by making it a scarce commodity. Rather, they were trying to protect unsuspecting people from its power which was the equivalent of an open flame. In the hands of dilettantes, it would burn the user and those near them. But when practiced by a master, Kabbalah could provide light and warmth.

The reasons for the danger are obvious when you understand the functioning principle of Kabbalistic thought. Without the use of drugs, it can magnify and intensify every part of life and thought. Like radar set to detect even the slightest movement, we can be so flooded by sensation and experience that we are unable to process them meaningfully. We focus on the negative because it is so magnified that it becomes all we see. Properly managed, though, this sensitivity can let us see potential in people and situations, to focus clearly on what's around us. But more data about our world and our lives are not necessarily welcome if we have no method to sort it all and convert it into knowledge.

Kabbalists believed that when we reached a higher spiritual plateau, we gained a wisdom and a power to heal physical as well as spiritual ailments. Incantations and magical formulas, such as the Aramaic mantra *abracadabra*, were used by people of magic from many faiths to cure everything from a toothache to the common cold. Some believed that this word, later popularized in many children's stories, meant "the father, the son and the holy spirit" or was a corruption of the Hebrew words for "blessing," *bracha*, and for "word," *dabar*. The prescription had to be done so that first the whole word had to be written on the top line; then on each subsequent line the word had to be repeated with one letter less. Until finally at the very bottom of the triangle only one letter was left:

```
A B R A C A D A B R A
A B R A C A D A B R
A B R A C A D A B
A B R A C A D A
A B R A C A D
A B R A C A
A B R A C
A B R A
A B R
A B
A
```

Regardless, the ancients feared that these incantations might give the young and undisciplined enough knowledge about Kabbalah to be dangerous. The unstable might think it was based on sorcery, not belief. If the problem couldn't be cured with an immediate answer, incantation or spell, the immature might dwell even more on their own shortcomings, problems and pain. In a mundane sense, imagine the impact on the bald person who is already so conscious of his baldness that all he sees are people with full heads of hair. Or the overweight woman who lives in a world of flat tummies and well-proportioned waists. If the "magic" of mysticism fails to grow hair or reduce weight, will these people obsess even more? Instead of minimizing the negative, would just the opposite occur?

After all, fixating on the negative is not uncommon. Add a misunderstood belief system and facts might become meaningless and truth transformed into individual idiosyncrasies. The thin would suddenly see themselves as fat and would exercise, purge and diet. The person with a pimple would look into a mirror and see no other attribute—only a pimple. Even the absolutely normal person might start exaggerating what is missing and ignore the intrinsic good beneath the surface.

Spiritual Maturity Means a Problem Is a Potential Opportunity

A spiritually mature person, a true mystic, views all problems as potential. The spiritual mind turns negative energy into positive results.

Consider this story of a man whose attitude converted negatives into positives. Despite being five feet, four inches tall and weighing a rather spherical 220 pounds, Morty is a respected art dealer and is married to a strikingly beautiful, brilliant woman.

"When I met Morty for the first time, he was unimpressive to say the least," his wife says. "But after you talk to him for two minutes, you don't see short and you don't see fat. Far from it. When Morty opens up his mouth to talk, all you can see is this amazing, compassionate man. When he's talking to you, he makes you feel that you are the most beautiful, articulate, important person in the room. And I love him for that."

An art critic once explained Morty's success this way: "When he's speaking to people about a piece of art, he puts them inside the mind of the artist. He's so knowledgeable and articulate that he places them inside the time period in which the piece was created, and helps them explore each nuance of the work. His genius is that he makes everyone feel that they discovered these things on their own. He mesmerizes them, and then they couldn't care less whether he's short or tall, fat or skinny. All they see is this bright, urbane sophisticate who treats each person as if he or she were his gallery's most important client."

Morty himself offers this take on his success: "I was blessed with a good mind, good taste and a gift of gab. I make fun of my shortness, my weight and make the most of what I know about art by telling people good stories. I learned a long time ago that I can be whomever I care to be when I'm telling a good story. People will hear the story, not necessarily see the storyteller. My secret is to find wonderful stories in the art I'm selling and tell those stories as best I can while my clients look at the work. It also helps that I'm short enough not to block their view of the painting."

A Yiddish proverb might explain Morty's success: "When your only tool is a hammer, make every problem a nail." Mystics would note that Morty not only minimized what might have brought him pain, but that he found his spiritual center in the process. His ability to concentrate on his finer traits created positive energy around him.

Let Your Soul Catch Up with You

Habitually focusing our attention on our positive qualities rather than on what seem to be our failings requires much concentration. It may be difficult, but doing so is crucial for those who aspire to be spiritually centered. Being focused is the essence of spirituality because it raises our sensitivity level. Kabbalah literally means "receiving," and students of mysticism believe that Kabbalah is based on our ability to make our entire being receptive to the wisdom and the divine sparks that surround us and are within us.

The sudden flash of insight that creates opportunities, the inspiration that comes in the middle of the night, the vision that transforms an all-consuming question into an all-encompassing answer are examples of spiritual receptivity. When our antennae are up and our inner radar is finely tuned, we can receive signals that we might not have otherwise received. Our maturity and wisdom help us interpret them into answers that are useful to us.

An ancient African legend describes why it is difficult to concentrate and focus on life's mystical possibilities. It is the story of Yameel, the fastest messenger and most reliable runner on the African continent. Myths abounded about Yameel's swiftness of foot, his sense of direction and his uncanny ability to find any location, from the most remote tree in the jungle to the largest village. Tribal leaders marveled at his speed and recounted tales of his quick sprints through the bush from one village to another.

So it was very strange that a village elder should encounter the runner on the road one day standing almost motionless. He asked: "Why have you stopped in the middle of a mission?"

Yameel looked down at the man and answered: "I have been running so fast that I have left my soul behind. I am standing here waiting for it to catch up to me."

Many of us move so fast that we have to stop and give

our souls a chance to catch up to where we are. Whether by meditation, prayer, reciting a mantra, or just quietly walking in the woods, stopping ourselves is part of what we need to get ourselves in spiritual sync. The process is like calibrating an instrument or tuning a piano. The mystics felt that before we could be receptive to the possibilities of life, we had to be at peace within. Only then could we focus.

The Kabbalists realized that the best way to slow down and let our souls catch up involved meditation or, as they called it, *Devekut*. For centuries, meditative techniques were used for more than simple relaxation or stress reduction. They offered the ability to force everyday worry from the mind. By calming the concerns of the conscious mind, mystics could become one with the universe.

Some ancient scholars developed prayer wheels made of Hebrew prayers written in concentric circles. While trying to read the prayers, the reader would become mesmerized. Other scholars stared into the flame of a candle, believing they could dissipate their negative energy into the flame. Others stared for long periods into a basin of clear water to induce either a meditative or a hypnotic state.

Here are two techniques I encourage people to use, and that I use myself when I find that my body has outrun my soul. But first, two cautions: Never do these while operating machinery or driving a car. And some people may find that they don't work for them, although many will claim that 10 minutes of these meditations make them feel better than a good night's sleep.

- **Breathing meditation**

Sit in a comfortable straight-backed chair. Place your feet on the ground. Close your eyes, and become aware of your breathing. Spend three to five minutes relaxing. Tense your feet, count to five and relax. Tense your ankles, count to five, relax. Follow the same routine with your calves, your thighs, your stomach, your chest, arms and hands. Tense and relax your neck, your face and forehead. Finally, breathe deeply without consciously trying to alter the rhythm of your breathing. If your mind drifts, return your concentration to your breathing.

- **Counting or tones meditation**

Use the "tensing and relaxing" exercise described above. Then begin counting or saying key words aloud. Some people count to four in order to focus their mind as their breath goes in and out. Some prefer using words such as "God" or "love." For example, as you breath in, say "one"; as you breathe out, say "two." Jewish mystics used words like *"Hu"* (which means "he" in Hebrew), instead of the name of God. They would say the "h" while inhaling and the "ooo" upon exhaling.

According to the ancient mystics, meditation sharpens our ability to see that for which we should be thankful. Recall that Jewish tradition asks us to say one hundred blessings a day. Trying to see our blessings is most rewarding when our soul is in this highly receptive state. Saying thanks for anything makes us stop and become even more aware. As a Yiddish proverb says, "If you are going to be miserable when

156

you are sick, be thankful when you are well."

The blessings need not be enormous. They should be things we ordinarily overlook. A gentleman once told the Kotzker Rebbe that he had nothing for which to be thankful. His business was losing money; his wife had died; his son was not talking to him; and his house was too small.

"Take your thumb and index finger," the Rebbe directed the man. "Take a deep breath, and then place those fingers on your nose and squeeze to the point that you will not be able to breathe out. Do not breathe from your mouth."

As the man started to turn red, the Rebbe cautioned: "Do not take your fingers away until you cannot stand it any longer." Finally, the man released his grip and inhaled deeply. "Ah," the Rebbe concluded. "The air is what you most take for granted, and suddenly you are grateful to have it. Now, look at the rest of your life that same way and see all that you have taken for granted."

We might give thanks for:

Being able to see the sky and the stars.

Being able to see our children.

Having healthy, bright children.

Having loving, supportive spouses.

Being able to be with friends.

Being able to make new friends.

Being able to hear music.

Being able to hear birds sing.

Being able to hear great people speak.

Being able to understand what they say.

Getting in touch with the blessings of our lives connects us with our souls. If Kabbalah sensitizes and magnifies what it touches, then it will also build self esteem, self-worth and a sense of well-being from the positive bricks and mortar we derive from reciting our blessings.

Don't be afraid to write down these blessings. This gives them a concrete feeling in our minds and gives them life. Hanging the list where it can be seen can help our souls keep up with us as we move through the day.

"Giving Away" Gratitude Creates Wonder

There will be days, of course, when none of these methods work. So when all else failed, mystics made a most effective and enchanting recommendation: Give some gratitude away!

Telling someone how much they mean to us or the qualities we most admire about them creates wonderful feelings in both the giver of gratitude and the recipient. Being able to make people feel good about themselves makes us focus on something positive and forces us to look past ourselves. It magically does the same for the recipient of our compliment, who can focus on some personal strength and still feel gratitude toward us for pointing it out. This is a spiritual no-lose situation.

In *Chicken Soup for the Soul,* Jack Canfield and Mark Victor Hansen tell of Sister Helen Mrosla. Sister Helen, while teaching at Saint Mary's School in Morris, Minnesota, became enchanted with a third-grader named Mark Eklund. This mischievous little boy always got into trouble, but always thanked his teacher for correcting him or helping him learn the error of his ways.

In later years, when Sister Helen taught mathematics to

junior high students, Mark was again in her classroom. One Friday afternoon, she felt that her students were frustrated, not only with math but with themselves and each other. So she passed out sheets of paper with a list of everyone in the class and asked each student to think of the nicest thing they could say about each classmate and write these next to the classmate's name.

Over the weekend, Sister Helen compiled what the students had said. At the start of Monday's class, each student received a list of his or her own best qualities, as judged by their classmates. As the students read their lists, the tone of the class changed dramatically. There was laughter and lightness.

Many years later, Mark Eklund was killed in action while serving with U.S. forces in Vietnam. After attending the funeral, Sister Helen and many of Mark's former classmates went to his parent's home to express their regrets. Mark's mother and father handed his former teacher a small slip of paper that had been found in Mark's wallet after he was killed. The paper had been folded and refolded so many times that bits of yellowing tape held it together. Without even having to look, the nun knew what the battered paper was.

As Mark's former classmates gathered around and noticed the faded sheet, a marvelous thing happened. Each recalled how they had kept their own sheet of paper long after they'd left Sister Helen's junior high school math class. Some carried it with them every day, as Mark had. Others had taped it into albums or framed it on a dresser. That moment so long ago, when scores of positive feelings flooded the hearts of Sister Helen's students, had also repaired a small corner of the world, bringing with it hope, comfort and courage. It had turned an ordinary day of junior high school math into something mystical.

Exercises for the Soul

Monday   Set your alarm clock 20 minutes ahead of your normal wake-up time. Use the extra few moments to slow down so you can avoid rushing into your day.

Tuesday   During your daily shower, close your eyes and try to feel each drop of water strike your face. Don't think about the day ahead or all the work to be done. Just concentrate on the warm water striking you.

Wednesday   Every two hours during your work day, take a two-minute breathing break. Slow down and concentrate on your breath as it moves in and out of your body.

Thursday   Rearrange and personalize your work space. Buy a new pen. Get flowers. Change the items posted to your bulletin board.

Friday   At some point during the day, take a "scenic break." Find the best vista from your home or office and look at it, or take a short walk through an outdoor area so nature's beauty can briefly touch you.

Saturday   Pray, silently or otherwise, for no less than ten or fifteen minutes.

Sunday   Take a hot, soothing bath for at least 30 minutes.

CHAPTER 12

PURSUING HAPPINESS

Imagine a large room without lights. Frayed electric wires dangle from the ceiling and walls, and sparks arc menacingly. Now, imagine that we're standing at the door of this room. Something we desperately want is in it, but it is hidden in the darkness. What should we do?

Some would be too afraid to cross the threshold. Others might enter, but stand immobile in a safe corner. Many would wait for someone they believed to be braver, richer, smarter or somehow better equipped to cope with the situation. When that person comes along, they follow. A few gifted people would know how to connect the wires to create power and light. Some of these would illuminate a section of the room to find a treasure, others would light the entire room so everyone could see.

Most of us are walking through a life that's very much like that dark, dangerous room. As a Yiddish proverb says, "The world is full of surprises, very few of which are pleasant." The mystics believed that our lives and our world were a bundle of sparks, some powered by our minds, others by our souls, and still others by the everyday world around us. Some were good, some bad, some without value. If we try to exploit the power in these sparks without thought, we will receive painful shocks...or worse. The mystics were convinced that even when the sparks jolt us, they produce enough light to give us a glimpse of the world. In that moment, we can gather some of the sparks together and the combinations will permanently illuminate a small part of our lives. Each time we create new light, we see more. Eventually we discover the treasures that surround us. If we let the sparks fly without trying to make connections, their power will be not only useless, but their energy may be negative and could injure or kill us.

Kabbalistic thinking is a way to harness those energy fields of our inner and outer worlds. Its adherents created meticulous blueprints to explain and alter the mind and spirit centuries before the discipline of psychology was born, and shrouded their enigmatic formulas with esoteric blessings, magical incantations and cryptic detail.

Some people don't need these ancient wisdoms to do well in life. They intuitively discover the blueprints for happiness on their own. They use the adversity and the negative energy they encounter as a basis for creating joy, as the power source to illuminate more of the world.

A wonderful example of such a person is the late George Burns. When his wife and comedic partner, Gracie Allen, died, everyone was convinced that his professional life was over. After all, he was 68 years old and had never been the star of the show. Gracie was. He was her straight man. Their act was based on their marriage, their family and friends and, most importantly, on Gracie's feigned naiveté.

But Burns began a new career that made him a greater star than before. He did not try to replace his wife or duplicate their act. Instead, he created routines about the silliness, memories and sensitivities of old age. By mixing whimsy with wisdom and sarcasm, he made his audience into what he once was: A straight man.

Burns took the "dangling wires" of his inner and outer world and connected them in a unique pattern that essentially reinvented his life. In his last decades, Burns seemed to be an even stronger comedian without Gracie. Although he missed her, he believed that every time he mentioned her name to an audience, her magic was still with him.

Connecting Sparks that Unite Mind, Body and Soul

We get our resilience and our creativity from faith. Every religious denomination and every culture has a different way to achieve the meaning and goodness that give us the tenacity and stamina to keep getting up when life knocks us down.

Regardless of our religious beliefs, the ideas and techniques of Jewish mysticism can be invaluable in helping us live the lives we want. Each mystical idea discussed in this book connects the sparking wires in the dark rooms that are our lives. By doing so we give ourselves more energy to achieve the happiness that God wants us to have.

Ancient scholars used illustrations to help explain these mystical ideas and show connections between body and soul.

165

Another way to make them practical to use in everyday life is to take the traditional materials and creatively interpret them. Then we can reduce them to equations and formulas, the way a mathematician might. But before we apply any formulas, we must define a personal and reasonable definition of joy. To do so:

- First write down what makes you happy. Is it a whim or is it truly what you want more than anything else in life?
- Craft a plan for every day that includes as much as possible of what makes you happy.
- As you live that plan your *B'shert*, or your road map, will emerge because you will be sensitized to the opportunities that await you. The wonderful mystery of life lies in your willingness to discover it.
- Once you discover an opportunity, seize it and adjust your course.

Melding Mind and Soul

The mystics drafted this formula for those of us who are cerebral. It lets emotion and intellect merge and take control of the body. Common sense *(Hokhmah)* and the rational analysis of the facts *(Binah)* combine and create action. That is why the formula is:

Hokhmah, wisdom, intuition or common sense +
Binah, understanding or facts and reason =
Daat, or knowing what to do through mind and body acting in concert.

Hokhmah: Mystics believe that this kind of wisdom emanates from the soul. It is both a spiritual and passionate response based on emotion, intuition and experience. If we just use *Hokhmah* without any reason, facts or knowledge we create a mindless spiritualism, a New Age fad.

Binah: This is a product of the mind. It is hard facts meeting rational thought. If we have facts and reason without intuition or common sense, then all we will really possess is a lifeless scientific form of thinking. One without the other is probably why some people who are spiritually oriented appear flaky and irrational and so many who are bean counters seem dense and unfeeling.

Daat: Imagine combining fact and imagination and mind and soul. The result is imagination and creativity in a practical form.

Make Things Go Right

This activity-based strategy helps us fight the excuses that get in the way of our joy. It helps us set reachable goals without interference. It also teaches us to be intolerant of the notion of perfection. It can be the key to success in any venture. The formula is:

Tiferet, or realistic goals +
Hod, or persistence =
Netzah, or conclusion.

Tiferet: Reasonable goal-setting creates a harmony that

is the best way to fight insatiability. By admitting that we can't possibly be the richest, the prettiest or the best, but that we can be *close* to the richest, the prettiest or the best, we open ourselves to the possibility of happiness. This type of attitude makes all of the difference in the world: Since impossible goals can never be reached, why make our goals unachievable?

Hod: Persistence is the key to getting what we want. Persistence is better than luck. Persistence is always in our control. Luck is not.

Netzah: Setting goals and not reaching them is self-destructive and cruel. One of the critical pieces of this equation is to come to conclusion. *Netzah* is the ability to say, "I'm done." We can't just win and walk away. Rather, we must take the time to appreciate what we have done. Every small victory adds to our sense of fulfillment and confidence. Enjoy this sense of wholeness, because feeling whole is a holy sensation. God meant us to feel that way. Once we have celebrated, closure becomes complete when we move on.

Being One with the World

This creates a sense of well-being for those who need healing or peace of mind. It combines opposites and relies on the principle that, while we may not be able to control the events that surround us, we can control our reaction to them. Or, as an English proverb says, "We cannot be master over the wind, but we can trim the sails." The formula is:

Gevurah, or strength +
Chesed, or grace =
Tiferet, or harmony.

Gevurah: Real strength comes from being able to control ourselves. This kind of power results from much practice and concentration. It is common to instinctively react to problems with anger, fear or inaction. Biologists call this the "fight or flight" response to danger. If we have true strength, though, we can control that instinctive reaction and thoughtfully respond to new challenges.

Chesed: Grace creates opportunities to do good things. Consciously finding the right way and the kindest way to handle situations and people produces an atmosphere of gentleness.

Tiferet: Harmony is the ability to feel at one with yourself and your world. It is the essence of well-being. The experience brings a sense of oneness and wholeness essential to a spiritual experience. By combining the strength of self-control and the willingness to create kindness with good deeds, we can experience a feeling that everything is well with our world.

Define Success...Then Succeed Happily

Many successful people think that their power, wealth or beauty makes them happy. But they are not, because their success is not defined. To avoid that trap, we must first define what we mean by success. Is it money? Is it fame? Is it some singular goal, such as hitting a baseball out of Wrigley

Field or playing with the New York Philharmonic? If we can specifically define our success before even pursuing it, and our goal is realistic, then this formula will lead to a success that brings happiness.

Hod, (splendor) or persistence +
Netzah, or conclusion +
Keva, or fixing set times =
Kavanah, or inspiration +
Yesod, (foundation) or attitude =
Success

Hod (persistence): Constantly chipping away at a project or problem is the foremost tool to achieve any objective. But remember that persistence is pointless without a goal.

Netzah (conclusion or overcoming all things and conditions): Don't let anyone stop you until you reach your goal. To create an atmosphere in which *Netzah* can thrive, break down all goals into smaller, more easily achievable results. If you want to lose 30 pounds, have secondary goals of 10 pounds and 20 pounds that let you celebrate along the way. When you overcome all obstacles and reach your major goal, pause, celebrate and move on with your life.

Keva ("fixing set times"): In order to keep getting results, keep at your work day after day, at the same time. If you are studying to become an expert in your profession, do it every day at the same time to get into the *Keva*, a "fixed habit."

Kavanah ("inspiration"): The result of your persistence is inspiration, that flash of genius and ingenuity that makes the complex simple. It occurs while you are thinking and working toward your pre-set goals.

Yesod ("attitude"): By adding the right frame of mind, all the pieces of the formula come together in a sensible way. *Yesod* is the spark plug, the will to win. It makes us believe in ourselves and our goals.

Repairing Your World

Centuries ago, an extremely wise rabbi lived near a monastery in the forest adjacent to a small English village. The abbot who led this group of monks for thirty years was discouraged. The monastery had once been an oasis for all to see the beauty of religious life. The buildings were now rundown, the orchards were overgrown. Only 20 old men remained in the order. All were miserable.

Brother Gregory and Brother Steven were constantly bickering. Brother Edward, who had once been a legendary cook, could no longer bake bread without burning it. The choirmaster complained that the monks no longer sang as well as they had in the past, and the monks murmured that the choirmaster was almost deaf. Brother Oscar and Brother Robert always argued over insignificant points of religious law and Brother Albert, once thought of as a philosopher, could only be counted on for cynicism.

These problems seemed insurmountable. In the midst of the abbot's depression, he remembered that a wise rabbi lived on the other side of the forest. Perhaps, as a last resort, he could help them.

The abbot visited the rabbi and told him about the

monastery's decline. "Because you are not one of us," the abbot said, "you might see the way to solve our problems." A few days later, the rabbi came to stay with the monks. He listened as they prayed and watched as they went about their daily routine. On the night of his planned departure, he told the abbot what he had seen during his visit.

"I have no idea how you can save this old building," the rabbi said. "And I really don't know what you will be able to do to rescue your order. But this I can tell you: One of you here is the Messiah, and that is far more important than your religious order or your building."

The abbot rang the bell in the tower of the monastery and awoke his colleagues, who ran to the chapel. "The rabbi has no advice to give to save our building or our order," the abbot began. The monks groaned and grumbled about why they had been awakened in the middle of the night for bad news. The abbot silenced them. "Before you go back to bed, I want you to know that the rabbi is sure of just one thing. He is positive that one of us is the Messiah. That is what I wanted to tell you."

There was a stunned silence. The monks returned to their chambers, but not one fell asleep.

"It is the choirmaster," Brother Frederick thought. "That's why he wants us to chant our prayers so loudly. He probably can hear as well as any of us. He just pretends he's deaf, so he has an excuse to make us better."

"It's the cook," the abbot realized. "He wants us to eat less and live longer. He could have made even more of those tasty treats he once prepared, but he knew we were all getting old and didn't need the extra food."

"It's got to be Brother Robert," Brother Oscar mused. "He disagrees with me about every subject so that I will always see the other point of view. How could I have been so blind not to see what he was doing and who he really is." Meanwhile, Brother Robert was sure that Oscar was the Holy One, for the exact same reason, and Brother Gregory was convinced that the Messiah "could be anybody, even Brother Albert. He's so testy and angry all the time because of his illnesses, but all he wants to do is make me more understanding of the infirm the world over."

Every monk had a suspicion that the abbot himself was the Messiah. Why else would the rabbi tell him, if not to reveal to him his true nature. After all, the abbot had put up with so much and had given so much of himself to make sure the monastery would remain viable.

In the weeks that followed, the monks were kinder to each other and more understanding. "After all," they assured themselves, "I know that I am not the Messiah because I have been so mean these past few years. But now, God has given me this chance to know the Messiah, face-to-face. I will not miss this opportunity."

Some monks, ashamed that the Messiah had been living in such a run-down, depressing place, made the grounds beautiful again, and the old monks began working with each other and doing chores that had gone undone for years.

When strangers wandering through the forest happened upon the monastery, they were amazed at the hospitality they received, the superb food they were served, the extraordinary wine and the melodious prayers that filled the air. Word spread of this wonderful place in the woods, and young men again began committing themselves to the order in the hope that they could spend their lives among such holy people. A miracle had happened: Happiness had returned to the monastery.

The Jewish mystics taught that happiness wasn't given to somebody who had everything. Instead, happy people had to be willing to give, to build a structure of kindness by making the people around them feel charity and understanding. By unknowingly performing *tikkun olam*, they repaired a small part of their world and their lives.

Happiness Is...

What then is happiness?

According to William Henry Channing, a Protestant clergyman who was chaplain to the U.S. Senate in the mid-nineteenth century, to be happy is "to live content with small means, to seek elegance rather than luxury, and refinement rather than fashion; to be worthy, not respectable; and wealthy, not rich; to study hard, think quietly, talk gently, act frankly; to listen to the stars and birds, to babes and sages, with open heart; to bear all cheerfully, do all bravely, await occasion, hurry never. In a word, to let the spiritual, unbidden and unconscious, grow up through the common."

Happiness means:

Accepting ourselves as we are.

Accepting the fact that we are vulnerable and can be hurt.

Accepting that all of us will fail, at times.

Accepting that, in order to be happy, we need to take risks.

No matter how frightened we are that failure will lead to embarrassment, no matter how terrified we are by the chance that love will lead to rejection and loneliness, no matter how weak we feel because of loss, we must accept these things and take a chance. A chance on ourselves, on our happiness, on the good people around us who dwell in the small corner of the world we have defined as our lives.

What else can we really do?

What choice do we really have?

Bahir: The Book of Brilliance, which was anonymously written and first surfaced in Provence, France, circa 1175.

Binah: Essential knowledge. Understanding which comes from three sources: The brain, research and ability. One of the ten **Sefirot.**

B'shert: A predestined path that is shaped by a combination of God's will and our own receptiveness to opportunity. Over the course of a life, it will take us in directions not initially seen or anticipated.

Hokhmah: Essential wisdom and common sense derived from the soul. One of the ten **Sefirot.**

Chesed: Grace; consciously finding a way to handle all situations with gentleness and kindness. One of the ten **Sefirot.**

Daat: A combination of wisdom and knowledge. This is the sum total of **Hokhmah** and **Binah** and produces the ability to make good things happen.

Devekut: One's inward fusing to the divine.

Gevurah: Strength; the ability to control one's passions. One of the ten **Sefirot.**

Gilgulim: The cycles or transformations of each soul's journey toward complete enlightenment. This concept presupposes a belief in reincarnation.

Hekhalot: The heavenly halls glimpsed during meditations practiced by Jewish mystics.

Hitlahavut: An overwhelming enthusiasm for the divine in every aspect of life.

Hod: "Splendor"; or more liberally, "Persistence." One of the ten **Sefirot**.

Kabbalah: Literally, "receiving." Generally used as a name for all Jewish mysticism. Essentially, it refers to an esoteric Jewish philosophy from the late 12th century onward.

Kabbalist: A student and practitioner of **Kabbalah**.

Kavanah: Mental concentration. The understanding of intent necessary for higher dimensions of awareness.

Kavvanoth: The name for meditation exercises developed by Kabbalists. These involve complex visualizations connected to the **Sefirot**.

Kelipot: Forces or "shells" of impurity that were the by-products of the creation of the world. Each person has the duty to heal the **Kelipot** found in daily life.

Keter: The crown of the **Sefirot**. Regarded as the true and most permeating force in the cosmos.

Keva: The act of setting aside a fixed time.

Malkhut: Presence. The kingdom or the lowest form of the ten **Sefirot**. This is what I call "success." The Kabbalist regards it as the passive, receptive force in the cosmos.

Neshamah: The soul or non-physical, transcendent part of a being that survives physical death.

Netzah: Victory. The ability to come to closure. One of the ten **Sefirot**.

Rebbe: Hasidic term for spiritual teacher and/or leader.

Sefer Yetzirah: The Book of Creation. It was anonymously written at some time between the third and sixth centuries C.E. (The earliest metaphysical text in Hebrew.)

Sefirot: The ten essential forms of energy that comprise the universe. The **Sefirot** historically have been portrayed in various arrangements, from a body of a king to a tree of life. In ascending order, they are:

Presence/Success (**Malkhut**).

Foundation/Attitude (**Yesod**).

Splendor/Persistence (**Hod**).

Eternity/Conclusion (**Netzah**).

Harmony (**Tiferet**).

Strength (**Gevurah**).

Grace (**Chesed**).

Reason (**Binah**).

Intuition, Common Sense, Wisdom (**Hokhmah**).

A higher nature of being (**Keter**).

Shekhinah: The feminine side of God.

Talmud: A compilation of Jewish oral law completed in 500 C.E. Two different recensions of the Talmud were written by sages in both Palestine and Babylon.

Tiferet: Harmony. The ability to feel at one with the universe by creating and experiencing realistic goals that can be imagined. One of the ten **Sefirot.**

Tikkun (also known as **Tikkún Olam**): Repairing the world. Every human act either aids or impedes this process.

Torah: Technically, the Five Books of Moses. In a wider sense, Torah is understood to comprise the 24 books of the Hebrew Bible and the Talmud, as well as the entire scope of Jewish teaching.

Tree of Life: The pivotal metaphor for the universe and every facet of it.

Tzimtzum: The contraction which took place during the

creation of the world and caused the shattered sparks of the universe that are the source good and evil. Alternatively, the chaotic, ambivalent push-and-pull of the universe.

Yesod: "Foundation" or for our purposes "Attitude" and the will to persevere. One of the ten **Sefirot**.

Yetzer Hara: The evil inclination that drives us toward envy, scorn, divisiveness and other negative traits and the immediate gratification of physical passions.

Yetzer Hatov: The good inclination. A positive predisposition that centers on the intellect and a conscious effort to remain mentally and spiritually balanced.

Zohar: The Book of Splendor. An essential text of Kabbalistic thought which first appeared in Spain in the late thirteenth century and though attributed to Rabbi Shimon bar Yochai, was probably composed by Moses de Leon.

Ariel, David. *The Mystic Quest: An Introduction to Jewish Mysticism.* New York: Schocken, 1992.

Bachya, ben Joseph ibn Paquada. *Duties of the Heart,* volumes 1 and 2. Translated by Moses Hyamson. Jerusalem: Feldheim, 1978.

Bindler, Paul. "Meditative Prayer and Rabbinic Perspectives on Psychology of Consciousness: Environmental, Physiological and Attentional Variables." *Journal of Psychology and Judaism,* Summer 1980, 4 (4), 228–248.

Blumenthal, David R. *Understanding Jewish Mysticism.* New York: Ktav, 1978.

Bokser, Ben Zion, editor. *The Jewish Mystical Tradition.* Northvale, N.J.: Jason Aronson, 1993.

Dan, Joseph, editor, and Ronald C. Kiener, translator. *The Early Kabbalah. The Classics of Western Spirituality.* Mahwah, N.J.: Paulist Press, 1986.

Green, Arthur, editor. *Jewish Spirituality. Volume 1: From the Bible through the Middle Ages. Volume 2: From the Sixteenth-Century Revival to the Present.* New York: Crossroad, 1986, 1988.

Halevi, Z'ev ben Shimon. *Adam and the Kabbalistic Tree.* New York: Weiser, 1974.

Halevi, Z'ev ben Shimon. *Kabbalah.* New York: Thames and Hudson, 1980.

Hoffman, Edward. "The Kabbalah: Its Implications for Humanistic Psychology." *Journal of Humanistic Psychology,* Winter 1980, 20 (1), 33–47.

Idel, Moshe. *Kabbalah: New Perspectives*. New Haven: Yale University Press, 1988.

Jacobs, Louis. *Hasidic Prayer*. New York: Schocken, 1978.

_____. *Jewish Mystical Testimonies*. New York: Schocken, 1977.

Kaplan, Aryeh, translator. *Bahir*. New York: Weiser, 1980.

_____. *Meditation and Kabbalah*. York Beach, Maine: Samuel Weiser, 1982.

Kushner, Lawrence. *Honey from the Rock*. Woodstock, Vt.: Jewish Lights, 1990.

Liebes, Yehuda. *Studies in the Zohar*. Albany: State University of New York Press, 1993.

Matt, Daniel C. *The Essential Kabbalah: The Heart of Jewish Mysticism*. San Francisco: HarperSanFrancisco, 1995.

_____. *God & the Big Bang: Discovering Harmony Between Science & Spirituality*. Woodstock, Vt.: Jewish Lights, 1996.

_____, editor and translator. *Zohar: The Book of Enlightenment*. *The Classics of Western Spirituality*. Mahwah, N.J.: Paulist Press, 1983.

Patai, Raphael. *The Hebrew Goddess*. Detroit: Wayne State University Press, 1990.

Rosten, Leo. *Treasury of Jewish Quotations*. New York: McGraw Hill, 1972.

Schachter–Shalomi, Zalman M. *Gate to the Heart*. Philadelphia: ALEPH, Alliance for Jewish Renewal, 1993.

Scholem, Gershom. *Kabbalah*. Jerusalem: Keter, 1974.

_____. *Major Trends in Jewish Mysticism*. New York: Schocken, 1961.

_____. *On the Kabbalah and Its Symbolism.* New York: Schocken, 1965.

_____. *On the Mystical Shape of the Godhead.* New York: Schocken, 1991.

_____. *Origins of the Kabbalah.* Philadelphia: Jewish Publication Society, 1987.

Sperling, Harry, and Maurice Simon, translators. *Zohar,* volumes 1–5. London: Soncino Press, 1931–1934.

Steinsaltz, Adin. Yehuda Hanegbi, translator. *The Thirteen Petalled Rose.* New York: Basic Books, 1980.

Tishby, Isaiah and Fischel Lachower. *The Wisdom of the Zohar: An Anthology of Texts.* Oxford: Oxford University Press, 1989.

Wolfson, Elliot R. *Along the Path: Studies in Kabbalistic Myth, Symbolism, and Hermeneutics.* Albany: State University of New York Press, 1995.

Unterman, Alan. *The Wisdom of the Jewish Mystics.* New York: New Directions, 1976.

For People of All Faiths, All Backgrounds

ABOUT JEWISH LIGHTS PUBLISHING

People of all faiths and backgrounds yearn for books that attract, engage, educate and spiritually inspire.

Our principal goal is to stimulate thought and help all people learn about who the Jewish People are, where they come from, and what the future can be made to hold. While people of our diverse Jewish heritage are the primary audience, our books speak to people in the Christian world as well and will broaden their understanding of Judaism and the roots of their own faith.

We bring to you authors who are at the forefront of spiritual thought and experience. While each has something different to say, they all say it in a voice that you can hear.

Our books are designed to welcome you and then to engage, stimulate and inspire. We judge our success not only by whether or not our books are beautiful and commercially successful, but by whether or not they make a difference in your life.

We at Jewish Lights take great care to produce beautiful books that present meaningful spiritual content in a form that reflects the art of making high quality books. Therefore, we want to acknowledge those who contributed to the production of this book.

PRODUCTION
Maria O'Donnell

EDITORIAL & PROOFREADING
Sandra Korinchak

BOOK & COVER DESIGN
Glenn Suokko, Woodstock, Vermont

TYPE
Set in Galliard
Glenn Suokko, Woodstock, Vermont

COVER PRINTING
Coral Graphics, Hicksville, New York

PRINTING AND BINDING
Book Press, Brattleboro, Vermont

Spirituality

MINDING THE TEMPLE OF THE SOUL
Balancing Body, Mind & Soul through Traditional Jewish Prayer, Movement & Meditation
by *Dr. Tamar Frankiel* and *Judy Greenfeld*

This new spiritual approach to physical health introduces readers to a spiritual tradition that affirms the body and enables them to reconceive their bodies in a more positive light. Relying on Kabbalistic teachings and other Jewish traditions, it shows us how to be more responsible for our own psychological and physical health. Focuses on the discipline of prayer, simple Tai Chi-like exercises and body positions, and guides the reader throughout, step by step, with diagrams, sketches and meditations.

7 x 10, 144 pp (est), Quality Paperback Original, illus., ISBN 1-879045-64-8 **$15.95**

BEST REFERENCE BOOK OF THE YEAR

HOW TO BE A PERFECT STRANGER
A Guide to Etiquette in Other People's Religious Ceremonies, Vol. 1
Edited by *Arthur J. Magida*

Explains the rituals and celebrations of America's major religions/denominations, helping an interested guest to feel comfortable, participate to the fullest extent possible, and avoid violating anyone's religious principles. **"A book that belongs in every living room, library and office."**

"The things Miss Manners forgot to tell us about religion."
— *Los Angeles Times*

AWARD WINNER

"Concise, informative, and eminently practical."
— *Rev. Christopher Leighton, Executive Director, Institute for Christian-Jewish Studies*

"Finally, for those inclined to undertake their own spiritual journeys...tells visitors what to expect."
—*The New York Times*

6 x 9, 432 pp. Hardcover, ISBN 1-879045-39-7 **$24.95**

COMING FALL '96: **VOL. 2: 20 ADDITIONAL FAITHS**
6 x 9, 432 pp (est), Hardcover, ISBN 1-879045-63-X **$24.95**

SPIRITUALITY...OTHER BOOKS:

Embracing the Covenant: Converts to Judaism Talk About Why & How
Edited by Rabbi Allan Berkowitz and Patti Moskovitz. 6 x 9, 192 pp, Quality Pb, ISBN 1-879045-50-8 $15.95

Finding Joy: A Practical Spiritual Guide to Happiness
by Dannel Schwartz with Mark Hass. 6 x 9, 192 pp, HC, ISBN 1-879045-53-2 $19.95

Tormented Master: The Life and Spiritual Quest of Rabbi Nahman of Bratslav
by Arthur Green. 6 x 9, 408 pp, Quality Pb, ISBN 1-879045-11-7 $17.95

Your Word Is Fire: The Hasidic Masters on Contemplative Prayer
Edited & transl. by Arthur Green & Barry W. Holtz. 6 x 9, 152 pp, Quality Pb, ISBN 1-879045-25-7 $14.95

Spiritual Inspiration for Daily Living . . .

INVISIBLE LINES OF CONNECTION
Sacred Stories of the Ordinary
by *Lawrence Kushner*

Through his everyday encounters with family, friends, colleagues and strangers, Kushner takes us deeply into our lives, finding flashes of spiritual insight in the process. This is a book where literature meets spirituality, where the sacred meets the ordinary, and, above all, where people of all faiths, all backgrounds can meet one another and themselves. Kushner ties together the stories of our lives into a roadmap showing how everything "ordinary" is supercharged with meaning—*if* we can just see it.

"Does something both more and different than instruct—it inspirits. Wonderful stories, from the best storyteller I know."
— *David Mamet, playwright*

6 x 9, 160 pp. Hardcover, ISBN 1-879045-52-4 **$21.95**

THE BOOK OF WORDS
Talking Spiritual Life, Living Spiritual Talk
by *Lawrence Kushner*

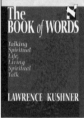

Kushner lifts up and shakes the dust off primary religious words we use to describe the spiritual dimension of life. The *Words* take on renewed spiritual significance, adding power and focus to the lives we live every day. For each word Kushner offers us a startling, moving and insightful explication, and pointed readings from classical Jewish sources that further illuminate the concept. He concludes with a short exercise that helps unite the spirit of the word with our actions in the world.

"It is wonderful! A surprise at every page. His translations and elaborations provoke and stimulate the religious imagination."

AWARD WINNER

—*Rabbi Neil Gillman, Chair, Dept. of Jewish Philosophy, Jewish Theologial Seminary*

6 x 9, 152 pp. Hardcover, beautiful two-color text ISBN 1-879045-35-4 **$21.95**

AWARD WINNER ## THE BOOK OF LETTERS
A Mystical Hebrew Alphabet
by *Lawrence Kushner*

In calligraphy by the author. Folktales about and exploration of the mystical meanings of the Hebrew Alphabet. Open the old prayerbook-like pages of *The Book of Letters* and you will enter a special world of sacred tradition and religious feeling. More than just symbols, all twenty-two letters of the Hebrew alphabet overflow with meanings and personalities of their own.

Rabbi Kushner draws from ancient Judaic sources, weaving Talmudic commentary, Hasidic folktales, and Kabbalistic mysteries around the letters.

"A book which is in love with Jewish letters." — *Isaac Bashevis Singer* (לז)

• **Popular Hardcover Edition** •
6 x 9, 80 pp. Hardcover, two colors, inspiring new Foreword.
ISBN 1-879045-00-1 **$24.95**

• **Deluxe Gift Edition** •
9 x 12, 80 pp. Hardcover, four-color text, ornamentation, in a beautiful slipcase.
ISBN 1-879045-01-X **$79.95**

• **Collector's Limited Edition** •
9 x 12, 80 pp. Hardcover, gold embossed pages, hand assembled slipcase. With silkscreened print.
Limited to 500 signed and numbered copies.
ISBN 1-879045-04-4 **$349.00**
To see a sample page at no obligation, call us

...*The Kushner Series*

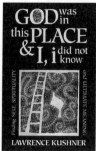

GOD WAS IN THIS PLACE & I, i DID NOT KNOW
Finding Self, Spirituality & Ultimate Meaning
by *Lawrence Kushner*

Who am I? Who is God? Kushner creates inspiring interpretations of Jacob's dream in Genesis, opening a window into Jewish spirituality for people of all faiths and backgrounds.

In a fascinating blend of scholarship, imagination, psychology and history, seven Jewish spiritual masters ask and answer fundamental questions of human experience.

"A brilliant fabric of classic rabbinic interpretations, Hasidic insights and literary criticism which warms us and sustains us."
—*Dr. Norman J. Cohen, Provost, Hebrew Union College*

"Rich and intriguing." —*M. Scott Peck, M.D., author of* The Road Less Traveled *and other books*

6 x 9, 192 pp. Quality Paperback, ISBN 1-879045-33-8 **$16.95**
6 x 9, 192 pp. Hardcover, ISBN 1-879045-05-2 **$21.95**

HONEY FROM THE ROCK
by *Lawrence Kushner*

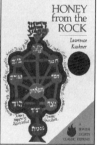

"Quite simply the easiest introduction to Jewish mysticism you can read."

An introduction to the ten gates of Jewish mysticism and how it applies to daily life.

"*Honey from the Rock* captures the flavor and spark of Jewish mysticism.... Read it and be rewarded." —*Elie Wiesel*

"A work of love, lyrical beauty, and prophetic insight. "
—*Father Malcolm Boyd*, The Christian Century

6 x 9, 168 pp. Quality Paperback, ISBN 1-879045-02-8 **$14.95**

THE RIVER OF LIGHT
Spirituality, Judaism, Consciousness
by *Lawrence Kushner*

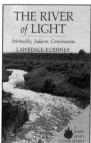

A "manual" for all spiritual travelers who would attempt a spiritual journey in our times. Taking us step by step, Kushner allows us to discover the meaning of our own quest: "to allow the river of light—the deepest currents of consciousness—to rise to the surface and animate our lives."

"Philosophy and mystical fantasy...exhilarating speculative flights launched from the Bible....Anybody—Jewish, Christian, or otherwise...will find this book an intriguing experience."
—*The Kirkus Reviews*

"A very important book."—*Rabbi Adin Steinsaltz*

6 x 9, 180 pp. Quality Paperback, ISBN 1-879045-03-6 **$14.95**

Spirituality

BEING GOD'S PARTNER
How to Find the Hidden Link
Between Spirituality and Your Work

by *Jeffrey K. Salkin* Introduction by *Norman Lear*

A book that will challenge people of every denomination to reconcile the cares of work and soul. A groundbreaking book about spirituality and the work world, from a Jewish perspective. Helps the reader find God in the ethical striving and search for meaning in the professions and in business. Looks at our modern culture of workaholism and careerism, and offers practical suggestions for balancing your professional life and spiritual self.

Being God's Partner will inspire people of all faiths and no faith to find greater meaning in their work, and see themselves doing God's work in the world.

"Will challenge not only Jews caught up in the hustle and the hassle...but everyone of whatever denomination concerned about making sense of our life and responding to the longings of the spirit within the soul."
— *Fr. Andrew M. Greeley, Prof. of Social Science, The University of Chicago*

"This engaging meditation on the spirituality of work is grounded in Judaism but is relevant well beyond the boundaries of that tradition."
— *Booklist*

6 x 9, 192 pp. Hardcover, ISBN 1-879045-37-0 **$19.95**

SELF, STRUGGLE & CHANGE
Family Conflict Stories in Genesis
and Their Healing Insights for Our Lives
by *Norman J. Cohen*

How do I find greater wholeness in my life and in my family's life?

The stress of late-20th-century living only brings new variations to timeless personal struggles. The people described by the biblical writers of Genesis were in situations and relationships very much like our own. We identify with them. Their stories still speak to us because they are about the same problems we deal with every day.

A modern master of biblical interpretation brings us greater understanding of the ancient text and of ourselves in this intriguing re-telling of conflict between husband and wife, father and son, brothers, and sisters.

"Delightfully written ... rare erudition, sensitivity and insight."
— *Elie Wiesel*

6 x 9, 224 pp. Hardcover, ISBN 1-879045-19-2 **$21.95**

THE EMPTY CHAIR: FINDING HOPE & JOY
Timeless Wisdom from a Hasidic Master,
Rebbe Nachman of Breslov

Adapted by *Moshe Mykoff* and *the Breslov Research Institute*

A "little treasure" of aphorisms and advice for living joyously and spiritually today, written 200 years ago, but startlingly fresh in meaning and use. Challenges and helps us to move from stress and sadness to hope and joy.

Teacher, guide and spiritual master—Rebbe Nachman provides vital words of inspiration and wisdom for life today for people of any faith, or of no faith. **AWARD WINNER**

"For anyone of any faith, this is a book of healing and wholeness, of being alive!"
— *Bookviews*

4 x 6, 128 pp., 2-color text, Deluxe Paperback, ISBN 1-879045-67-2 **$9.95**

Spirituality

GODWRESTLING—ROUND 2
Ancient Wisdom, Future Paths
by *Arthur Waskow*

This 20th anniversary sequel to a seminal book of the Jewish renewal movement deals with spirituality in relation to personal growth, marriage, ecology, feminism, politics, and more. Including new chapters on recent issues and concerns, Waskow outlines original ways to merge "religious" life and "personal" life in our society today.

BEST RELIGION BOOK OF THE YEAR

"A delicious read and a soaring meditation."
—*Rabbi Zalman M. Schachter-Shalomi*

AWARD WINNER "Vivid as a novel, sharp, eccentric, loud....An important book for anyone who wants to bring Judaism alive."
—*Marge Piercy*

6 x 9, 352 pp. Hardcover, ISBN 1-879045-45-1 **$23.95**

GOD & THE BIG BANG
Discovering Harmony Between Science & Spirituality
by *Daniel C. Matt*

Mysticism and science: What do they have in common? How can one enlighten the other? By drawing on modern cosmology and ancient Kabbalah, Matt shows how science and religion can together enrich our spiritual awareness and help us recover a sense of wonder and find our place in the universe.

"This poetic new book...helps us to understand the human meaning of creation."
—*Joel Primack, leading cosmologist, Professor of Physics, University of California, Santa Cruz*

6 x 9, 216 pp. Hardcover, ISBN 1-879045-48-6 **$21.95**

THEOLOGY & PHILOSOPHY

Aspects of Rabbinic Theology
by Solomon Schechter. 6 x 9, 440 pp, Quality Paperback, ISBN 1-879045-24-9 $18.95

The Earth Is the Lord's: The Inner World of the Jew in Eastern Europe
by Abraham Joshua Heschel. 5.5 x 8, 112 pp, Quality Paperback, ISBN 1-879045-42-7 $12.95

The Last Trial: On the Legends and Lore of the Command to Abraham to Offer Isaac as a Sacrifice
by Shalom Spiegel. 6 x 9, 208 pp, Quality Paperback, ISBN 1-879045-29-X $17.95

A Passion for Truth: Despair and Hope in Hasidism
by Abraham Joshua Heschel. 5.5 x 8, 352 pp, Quality Paperback, ISBN 1-879045-41-9 $18.95

Seeking the Path to Life: Theological Meditations on God and the Nature of People, Love, Life and Death
by Rabbi Ira F. Stone 6 x 9, 132 pp, Quality Paperback, ISBN 1-879045-47-8 $14.95;
HC, ISBN -17-6 $19.95

The Spirit of Renewal: Finding Faith After the Holocaust
by Edward Feld 6 x 9, 224 pp, Quality Paperback, ISBN 1-879045-40-0 $16.95
HC, ISBN -06-0 $22.95

Self-Help/Recovery

Healing of Soul, Healing of Body: Spiritual Leaders Unfold the Strength & Solace in Psalms
Edited by Rabbi Simkha Y. Weintraub, CSW for the Jewish Healing Center. 6 x 9, 2-color text, 128 pp,
Quality Paperback, ISBN 1-879045-31-1 $14.95

Twelve Jewish Steps to Recovery: A Personal Guide to Turning from Alcoholism & Other Addictions
by Dr. Kerry M. Olitzky & Stuart A. Copans, M.D. 6 x 9, 136 pp,
Quality Paperback, ISBN 1-879045-09-5 $13.95 HC, ISBN 1-879045-08-7 $19.95

Recovery from Codependence: A Jewish Twelve Steps Guide to Healing Your Soul
by Dr. Kerry M. Olitzky. 6 x 9, 160 pp,
Quality Paperback, ISBN 1-879045-32-X $13.95 HC, ISBN 1-879045-27-3 $21.95

Renewed Each Day: Daily Twelve Step Recovery Meditations Based on the Bible
by Dr. Kerry M. Olitzky & Aaron Z. Vol. I, Genesis & Exodus, 224 pp; Vol. II, Leviticus, Numbers &
Deuteronomy, 280 pp; Two-Volume Set, Quality Paperback, ISBN 1-879045-21-4 $27.90

*One Hundred Blessings Every Day: Daily Twelve Step Recovery Affirmations, Exercises for Personal
Growth & Renewal Reflecting Seasons of the Jewish Year*
by Dr. Kerry M. Olitzky. 4.5 x 6.5, 432 pp, Quality Paperback, ISBN 1-879045-30-3 $14.95

Lifecycle

Bar/Bat Mitzvah Basics: A Practical Family Guide to Coming of Age Together
Edited by Cantor Helen Leneman. 6 x 9, 224 pp,
HC, ISBN 1-879045-51-6 $24.95 Quality Pb, ISBN 1-879045-54-0 $16.95

Hanukkah by Dr. Ron Wolfson. 7 x 9, 192 pp, Quality Paperback, ISBN 1-870945-97-4 $16.95

Lifecycles, Vol. 1: Jewish Women on Life Passages & Personal Milestones
Edited by Rabbi Debra Orenstein. 6 x 9, 480 pp, HC, ISBN 1-879045-14-1 $24.95

Lifecycles, Vol. 2: Jewish Women on Biblical & Contemporary Life Themes
Ed. by Rabbi Debra Orenstein & Rabbi Jane Litman. 6 x 9, 480 pp,
HC, ISBN 1-879045-15-X $24.95 Available Nov. 1996

Mourning & Mitzvah: A Guided Journal to Walking the Mourner's Path Through Grief to Healing
by Anne Brener. 7.5 x 9, 288 pp, Quality Paperback, ISBN 1-879045-23-0 $19.95

The New Jewish Baby Book: Names, Ceremonies, Customs—A Guide for Today's Families
by Anita Diamant. 6 x 9, 328 pp, Quality Paperback, ISBN 1-879045-28-1 $15.95

The Passover Seder by Dr. Ron Wolfson. 7 x 9, 336 pp,
Quality Paperback, ISBN 1-879045-93-1 $16.95

*Putting God on the Guest List, 2nd Edition: How to Reclaim the Spiritual Meaning of Your Child's
Bar or Bat Mitzvah* by Jeffrey K. Salkin. 6 x 9, 232 pp,
Quality Paperback ISBN 1-879045-59-1 $16.95 HC ISBN 1-879045-58-3 $24.95

The Shabbat Seder by Dr. Ron Wolfson. 7 x 9, 272 pp,
Quality Paperback, ISBN 1-879045-90-7 $16.95

So That Your Values Live On: Ethical Wills & How to Prepare Them
Edited by Jack Riemer & Nathaniel Stampfer. 6 x 9, 272 pp,
Quality Paperback, ISBN 1-879045-34-6 $16.95 HC, ISBN 1-879045-07-9 $23.95

A Time to Mourn, A Time to Comfort: A Guide to Jewish Bereavement and Comfort
by Dr. Ron Wolfson. 7 x 9, 320 pp, Quality Paperback, ISBN 1-879045-96-6 $16.95

*When a Grandparent Dies: A Kid's Own Remembering Workbook for
Dealing with Shiva and the Year Beyond* by Nechama Liss-Levinson, Ph.D. 8 x 10, 2-color text, 48 pp,
HC, ISBN 1-879045-44-3 $14.95

Children's

BUT GOD REMEMBERED
Stories of Women from Creation to the Promised Land
by *Sandy Eisenberg Sasso*

Full color illustrations by *Bethanne Andersen*

NONSECTARIAN, NONDENOMINATIONAL.
A fascinating collection of four different stories of women only briefly mentioned in biblical tradition and religious texts, but never before explored. Award-winning author Sasso brings to life the intriguing stories of Lilith, Serach, Bityah, and the Daughters of Z, courageous and strong women from ancient tradition. All teach important values through their faith and actions.

For ages 8 and up

"Exquisite....a book of beauty, strength and spirituality."
—Association of Bible Teachers

9 x 12, 32 pp. Hardcover, Full color illus., ISBN 1-879045-43-5 **$16.95**

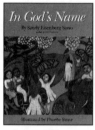

IN GOD'S NAME
For ages 4-8
by *Sandy Eisenberg Sasso*
Full color illustrations by *Phoebe Stone*

MULTICULTURAL, NONSECTARIAN, NONDENOMINATIONAL.
Like an ancient myth in its poetic text and vibrant illustrations, this modern fable about the search for God's name celebrates the diversity and, at the same time, the unity of all the people of the world. Each seeker claims he or she alone knows the answer. Finally, they come together and learn what God's name really is, sharing the ultimate harmony of belief in one God by people of all faiths, all backgrounds.

AWARD WINNER

"I got goose bumps when I read *In God's Name,* its language and illustrations are that moving. This is a book children will love and the whole family will cherish for its beauty and power."
—Francine Klagsbrun, author of *Mixed Feelings*

"What a lovely, healing book!"
—Madeleine L'Engle

Selected by
Parent Council Ltd.™

9 x 12, 32 pp. Hardcover, Full color illus., ISBN 1-879045-26-5 **$16.95**

For ages 4-8

GOD'S PAINTBRUSH
by *Sandy Eisenberg Sasso*
Full color illustrations by *Annette Compton*

MULTICULTURAL, NONSECTARIAN, NONDENOMINATIONAL.
Invites children of all faiths and backgrounds to encounter God openly in their own lives. Wonderfully interactive, provides questions adult and child can explore together at the end of each episode.

"An excellent way to honor the imaginative breadth and depth of the spiritual life of the young."
—Dr. Robert Coles, Harvard University

AWARD WINNER

11 x 8½, 32 pp. Hardcover, Full color illustrations, ISBN 1-879045-22-2 **$16.95**

THE 11TH COMMANDMENT
Wisdom from Our Children
For all ages
by The Children of America

MULTICULTURAL, NONSECTARIAN, NONDENOMINATIONAL.

"If there were an Eleventh Commandment, what would it be?"
Children of many religious denominations across America answer this question—in their own drawings and words—in *The 11th Commandment*. This full-color collection of "Eleventh Commandments" reveals kids' ideas about how people should respond to God.

8 x 10, 48 pp. Hardcover, Full color illustrations, ISBN 1-879045-46-X **$16.95**

# of Copies	Order Information	$ Amount

# of Copies		$ Amount
_____	Aspects of Rabbinic Theology (pb), $18.95	_____
_____	Bar/Bat Mitzvah Basics (hc), $24.95; (pb), $16.95	_____
_____	Being God's Partner (hc), $19.95	_____
_____	But God Remembered (hc), $16.95	_____
_____	Earth is the Lord's (pb), $12.95	_____
_____	11th Commandment (hc), $16.95	_____
_____	Embracing the Covenant (pb), $15.95	_____
_____	Empty Chair (pb), $9.95	_____
_____	Finding Joy (hc), $19.95	_____
_____	God & the Big Bang (hc), $21.95	_____
_____	God's Paintbrush (hc), $16.95	_____
_____	Godwrestling—Round 2 (hc), $23.95	_____
_____	Hanukkah (pb), $16.95	_____
_____	Healing of Soul, Healing of Body (pb), $14.95	_____
_____	How to Be a Perfect Stranger Vol. 1 (hc), $24.95	_____
_____	How to Be a Perfect Stranger Vol. 2 (hc), $24.95	_____
_____	In God's Name (hc), $16.95	_____
_____	Last Trial (pb), $17.95	_____
_____	Lifecycles Volume 1 (hc), $24.95	_____
_____	Lifecycles Volume 2 (hc), $24.95	_____
_____	Minding the Temple of the Soul (pb), $15.95	_____
_____	Mourning & Mitzvah (pb), $19.95	_____
_____	New Jewish Baby Book (pb), $15.95	_____
_____	One Hundred Blessings Every Day (pb), $14.95	_____
_____	Passion for Truth (pb), $18.95	_____
_____	Passover Seder (pb), $16.95	_____
_____	Putting God on the Guest List (hc), $24.95; (pb), $16.95	_____
_____	Recovery from Codependence (hc), $21.95; (pb), $13.95	_____
_____	Renewed Each Day, 2-Volume Set (pb), $27.90	_____
_____	Seeking the Path to Life (hc), $19.95; (pb), $14.95	_____
_____	Self, Struggle & Change (hc), $21.95	_____
_____	Shabbat Seder (pb), $16.95	_____
_____	So That Your Values Live On (hc), $23.95; (pb), $16.95	_____
_____	Spirit of Renewal (hc), $22.95; (pb), $16.95	_____
_____	Time to Mourn, Time to Comfort (pb), $16.95	_____
_____	Tormented Master (pb), $17.95	_____
_____	Twelve Jewish Steps to Recovery (hc), $19.95; (pb), $13.95	_____
_____	When a Grandparent Dies (hc), $14.95	_____
_____	Your Word is Fire (pb), $14.95	_____
_____	Other:_____	

• The Kushner Series •

_____	Book of Letters (popular edition) (hc), $24.95	_____
_____	Book of Words (hc), $21.95	_____
_____	God Was in This Place...(hc), $21.95; (pb), $16.95	_____
_____	Honey From the Rock (pb), $14.95	_____
_____	Invisible Lines of Connection (hc), $21.95	_____
_____	River of Light (pb), $14.95	_____

Check enclosed for $_____ *payable to:* JEWISH LIGHTS Publishing

Charge my credit card: ❏ MasterCard ❏ Visa

Credit Card #_____ Expires _____

Name on card _____

Signature _____ Phone (_____)_____

Name _____

Street _____

City / State / Zip _____

Phone, fax, or mail to: JEWISH LIGHTS Publishing
P. O. Box 237, Sunset Farm Offices, Route 4, Woodstock, Vermont 05091
Tel (802) 457-4000   *Fax* (802) 457-4004
Credit card orders (800) 962-4544 (9AM–5PM ET Monday–Friday)
Generous discounts on quantity orders. SATISFACTION GUARANTEED. Prices subject to change.

AVAILABLE FROM BETTER BOOKSTORES. TRY YOUR BOOKSTORE FIRST.